Paul the Accused
His Portrait in the
Acts of the Apostles

Marie-Eloise Rosenblatt, R.S.M.

A Michael Glazier Book
THE LITURGICAL PRESS
Collegeville, Minnesota

Zacchaeus Studies: New Testament

General Editor: Mary Ann Getty

The Scripture quotations contained herein are from the Revised Standard Version Bible, Catholic Edition, copyright 1946, 1971, and 1982 by the Division of Christian Education of the National Council of Churches of Christ in the USA. Used by permission. All rights reserved.

A Michael Glazier Book published by The Liturgical Press.

Cover design by David Manahan, O.S.B.
Oil painting by Rembrandt van Rijn, *Paul in Prison,* 1627, Staatsgalerie, Stuttgart.

1   2   3   4   5   6   7   8

Library of Congress Cataloging-in-Publication Data

Rosenblatt, Marie-Eloise.
    Paul the accused : his portrait in Acts of the Apostles / Marie-Eloise Rosenblatt.
        p.   cm. — (Zacchaeus studies.   New Testament)
    "A Michael Glazier book."
    Includes bibliographical references.
    ISBN 0-8146-5750-8
    1. Paul, the Apostle, Saint.   2. Bible.   N.T.   Acts—Criticism, interpretation, etc.   I. Title.   II. Series.
BS2506.R67   1995
225.9′2—dc20   94-16103
                                                              CIP

For David Daube

Contents

Editor's Note

Zacchaeus Studies provide concise, readable, and relatively inexpensive scholarly studies on particular aspects of Scripture and theology. The New Testament section of the series presents studies dealing with focal or debated questions; the volumes focus on specific texts or particular themes of current interest in biblical interpretation. Specialists have their professional journals and other forums where they discuss matters of mutual concern, exchange ideas, and further contemporary trends of research; some of their work on contemporary biblical research is now made accessible for students and others in *Zacchaeus Studies*.

The authors in this series share their own scholarship in nontechnical language, in the areas of their expertise and interest. These writers stand with the best in current biblical scholarship in the English-speaking world. Since most of them are teachers, they are accustomed to presenting difficult material in comprehensible form without compromising a high level of critical judgment and analysis.

The works of this series are ecumenical in content and purpose and cross credal boundaries. They are designed to augment formal and informal biblical study and discussion. Hopefully they will also serve as texts to enhance and supplement seminary, university, and college classes. The series will also aid Bible study groups, adult education, and parish religious education classes to develop intelligent, versatile, and challenging programs for those they serve.

Mary Ann Getty
New Testament Editor

Acknowledgments

The research for this study on the portrait of Paul in Acts of the Apostles began in the early 1980s at the École Biblique et Archéologique Française in Jerusalem, Israel. In 1987, it culminated in a doctoral dissertation at the Graduate Theological Union in Berkeley, California, and was entitled, *Under Interrogation: Paul as Witness in Juridical Contexts in Acts and the Implied Spirituality for Luke's Community.* The present volume is a synthesis of the argument of that dissertation directed by Professor John R. Donahue, S.J., of the Jesuit School of Theology at the Graduate Theological Union in Berkeley, with support from Professor William Herzog III of the American Baptist School of the West, Frank Houdek, S.J., of the Jesuit School, and close reading by Professor David Daube of Boalt Law School, Berkeley.

The National Conference on Christians and Jews in New York, in collaboration with the Shalom Hartman Institute, sponsored a series of three international study conferences in Jerusalem which brought together Jewish and Christian scholars. My perspective in this volume has been influenced by discussions of several weeks' duration in 1984 and 1986 under the direction of Professors David Hartman, Paul Van Buren, and Tzvi Marx.

It has been my good fortune to have enjoyed for more than a decade the scholarly challenge of colleagues in the Catholic Biblical Association. Funding for the research of this volume was provided by Catholic Biblical Association Memorial Stipends. My thanks to Professors Dianne Bergant, C.S.A., John Eliott, Richard Clifford, S.J., and Joseph Jensen, O.S.B.

I wish to thank Père Bernard Couroyer, O.P., now deceased, Jerry Murphy-O'Connor, O.P., Benedict Viviano, O.P., and Justin Taylor, S.M., of the École Biblique who at various times called my attention to sources useful for this study; to Robert Comtois, O.P., Prior, and the faculty and staff of the École Biblique for their gracious welcome of this "ancien élève," and assistance on the occasion of several visits to Jerusalem.

Mary Ann Getty is a wise series editor who gave judicious direction at various points in revising the manuscript. Mark Twomey and Michael Naughton, O.S.B., of The Liturgical Press, were accessible and responsive. Ellen Fitzgerald, Ph.D., of the Sisters of Mercy in Burlingame, proofed the galleys. Subject indexing was done by AnnMarie Mitchell, Librarian for Romance Collections of Doe Library, University of California, Berkeley. Author and Scripture indexes were compiled by my research assistant at Santa Clara University, Therese Inkmann.

The translation of Scripture used in this volume is the RSV.

Introduction

There has always been debate about Luke's purpose in writing his two-volume composition, the Gospel and the Acts of the Apostles. Most theologians assume that the same author composed both texts, and they affirm the interconnectedness of themes common to Luke-Acts.[1] However, much exegetical literature and most commentaries on Acts have rested on either of two assumptions that control the interpretation of individual passages.

The first assumption involves the question of Luke's politics in Acts. What is his relationship to Rome? Who is he trying to persuade and for what reasons? Many scholars have assumed that Luke felt either friendly or cautious toward Roman authority but certainly protective toward the Church. According to this assumption, Paul is presented as a law-abiding citizen and a model representing other Christians. Like Paul, Christian communities

---

[1]See François Bovon, *Luke the Theologian: Thirty-Three Years of Research (1950–1983),* trans. Ken McKinney [*Luc le théologien* Neuchâtel-Paris, Delachaux & Niestlé, 1978] Princeton Theological Monograph Series 12 (Allison Park, Penn.: Pickwick Publications, 1987). This is a translation and revision of the French version, largely a survey of writing about Luke's theological themes: salvation history and eschatology, interpretation of Old Testament, Christology, Holy Spirit, salvation and its reception, and the Church. Bibliographies included European as well as English-language resources. Also useful is I. Howard Marshall, "The Present State of Lucan Studies," *Themelios* 14 (January–February 1989) 52–56. The author is himself a commentator on Acts who regards Luke as historically reliable. His selective survey touches on major theological themes in mostly English-language works published mainly between 1970 and 1987.

might be resisted or criticized, but they are nonetheless innocent of wrongdoing. Luke writes Acts as a public address to Rome, designed to obtain clemency and acceptance for the Church.[2]

The second assumption is that the theological aim of Luke's narrative is to demonstrate God's revelation passing from Judaism to the Church. This aim is enhanced by portraying the resistance of Jews to the apostolic message. Luke's supposed emphasis on the superiority of the Church is proved by pointing out passages which show Gentiles accepting the gospel. According to this principle, presumed to represent the heart and mind of Luke, the narrative of Acts rests upon a rejection-affiliation model of evangelization.

These two older assumptions have governed descriptions of Luke's hero, Paul of Tarsus. Luke never gives a physical description of Paul in the biographical narrative.[3] Instead, the evangelist

---

[2]For an example of this perspective perduring in recent scholarship, see Philip Francis Esler, *Community and Gospel in Luke-Acts: The Social and Political Motivations of Lucan Theology,* Society for New Testament Studies Monograph Series 57 (Cambridge: Cambridge University Press, 1987, 1989). The author uses a redactional-sociological approach to describe the inclusiveness of the Christian community in its outreach to Gentiles, particularly in matters of table fellowship. He challenges the salvation-history model of Conzelmann, but stays within the more traditional assumption of Luke's supposed apologetic that Rome and Christianity were compatible.

[3]Abraham J. Malherbe, "A Physical Description of Paul," *Christians Among Jews and Gentiles: Essays in Honor of Krister Stendahl on His Sixty-Fifth Birthday,* ed. George W. E. Nickelsburg and George W. MacRae (Philadelphia: Fortress Press, 1986) 170–75. This physical description of Paul is given in the Acts of Paul and Thecla: "A man small of stature, with a bald head and crooked legs, in a good state of body, with eyebrows meeting and nose somewhat hooked, full of friendliness; for now he appeared like a man, and now he had the face of an angel." See E. Hennecke, *New Testament Apocrypha,* trans. Ernest Best and others. (Originally E. Hennecke, *Neutestamentliche Apokryphen,* Vol. 2, ed. Wilhelm Schneemelcher [Tübingen: J.C.B. Mohr/Paul Siebeck, 1964].) English translation: ed. R. McL. Wilson (London: Lutterworth Press/Philadelphia: Westminster Press, 1965). The phrase "he had the face of an angel" is on p. 354. Malherbe, 172, notes that the New Testament gives, typically, no physical description of its main characters. Paul's features of eyebrows meeting, a hook nose, and a small but well-made stature are quite attractive within the classical conventions

captures the portrait of the apostle's spiritual convictions, his intense missionary activity, and his memorable preaching.[4] Presumably, Paul's speeches and his court appearances serve Luke's apologetic aim of proving Paul's credentials as a loyal Roman citizen. When Paul encounters opposition on numerous occasions from Jewish authorities and synagogue hearers, this supposedly illustrates Luke's theological conviction. God's revelation has bypassed Judaism in favor of a Church which is now Gentile. A widely used theological term for the Church, the *new Israel,* is, however, not found in the New Testament itself.

Against these commonly held theses, *Paul the Accused* presents a different analytical perspective. This study of Paul subverts both these assumed theses. It attempts to refocus the portrait within lines which are faithful to the actual texts of Acts. For example, why has Luke placed emphasis on Paul as a prisoner and a defendant?[5] We observe that the last third of Acts is dominated by episodes of Paul's imprisonment and the texts of his defense speeches. If *witness,* a word often appearing in Acts, is a literal reference to the world of judges, legal procedures, and courtrooms, what are the implications of legal witness for Paul's overall portrait? How does this theme of witness control Paul's portrait?

---

of describing Augustus and Heracles, for example. Bowed legs make it easy to stand firmly planted.

[4]See Charles H. Talbert, "Biographies of Philosophers and Rulers as Instruments of Religious Propaganda in Mediterranean Antiquity," *Aufstieg und Niedergang der Römischen Welt* 2. 16. 2, ed. Wolfgang Haase (Berlin, N.Y.: De Gruyter, 1978) 1619–51. Talbert discusses the relation of the literary genre of the synoptic Gospels to Greco-Roman conventions used by classical authors. Even though there is no explicit discussion of Acts, Talbert's study has useful applications in contextualizing Luke's biographical portrait of Paul. Also useful is David E. Aune, *The New Testament in Its Literary Environment,* Library of Early Christianity (Philadelphia: Westminster Press, 1987). Two chapters focus on Luke-Acts: "Luke-Acts and Ancient Historiography" (77–115) and "Generic Features of Luke-Acts and the Growth of Apostle Literature" (116–57). The author provides well-focused bibliographies of both classical sources and current scholarship.

[5]The general perspective and assumptions of this study of Paul owe much to the scholarship of David Daube. See *Appeasement or Resistance and Other Essays on New Testament Judaism* (Berkeley: University of California Press, 1987).

Does it not reinforce his relationship with Peter and therefore his credibility as a missionary who preaches a gospel of inclusion for the Gentiles which the entire Church community endorses?

If we reinterpret Luke's political and theological perspective in light of a more synthetic reading of the narrative of Acts, we discover that he is preoccupied with recording the essential connection of the Church with its Jewish roots.[6] Paul remains a faithful Jew to the end, dedicated to a message which involves debates with other Jewish believers. Luke's theological purpose in Acts is not to show Paul's rejection of Jews and his subsequent embrace of Gentiles. Throughout Acts 13–28, Paul preaches to both Jewish and Gentile audiences. He is accepted and rejected by members of both groups.[7]

---

[6]James H. Charlesworth, *Paul and the Dead Sea Scrolls,* ed. J. Murphy-O'Connor and James H. Charlesworth (New York: Crossroad, 1990) x–xi. The heavily-biased tendencies of New Testament scholarship from 1835 to 1940 can be understood as related to "the beginnings of historical critical scholarship, the celebration of Greek ideas with the concomitant denigration of Jewish concepts, and the nonreflective anti-Semitic dimensions of Western triumphal Christianity" (x). Now, instead of being portrayed as a Jew only by birth who "thought like a Greek and wrote in Greek," Paul is seen "more as theocentric than christocentric . . . as a brilliant Jewish thinker, not a Greek scholar. He is comprehended in light of the Jewish apocalypses and other Jewish writings, especially the Dead Sea Scrolls."

[7]Joseph B. Tyson, *The Death of Jesus in Luke-Acts* (Columbia: University of South Carolina Press, 1986) 32. Luke 4:16-30, Jesus' sermon at Nazareth, is programmatic for the Gospel because it shows the response of the Jewish public to Jesus, and makes use of the literary pattern of initial acceptance followed by rejection. The pattern also applies to Luke-Acts as a whole. The treatment of the Jewish public, moving from acceptance to rejection, is more complex in Acts than in the Gospel. Richard J. Cassidy, *Society and Politics in the Acts of the Apostles* (Maryknoll, N.Y.: Orbis, 1987) 70–81, distinguishes various categories of Paul's non-Roman opponents, as reported in Acts. This identification requires the reader to avoid assuming a simplistic polarization between rejectionist Jews and accepting Gentiles. See his treatment of "Jewish-Law" Christians, Gentiles in Asia Minor and Greece, unbelieving Jews of the Diaspora, unbelieving Jews of Jerusalem, and chief priests and their Sanhedrin allies. This description also undercuts any assumption that Paul at some point abandoned his religious tradition and left Judaism "behind."

Nor is Luke's political purpose to prove to Roman authorities that Christianity is a religion which poses no threat to the empire. In countering this assumption about Luke's politics, Richard Cassidy has noted that officials of the Roman government in Acts are not really interested in the fortunes or religious message of a single prisoner from a politically troubled part of the empire. Their principal concerns are preservation of order, maintenance of secure frontiers, tax payments, commerce, transportation, and communication. They are not predisposed to give special consideration to the theological positions of spokespersons from a social minority who deviate from the Hellenistic mainstream. Luke, in fact, seems little concerned to canonize Roman officials, showing them as sometimes effective, often venal administrators.[8]

Dissatisfaction with the previous assessments of Luke's theology, politics, and portrait of Paul has grown in the last decade. Increased sensitivity of scholars to theological issues in the New Testament has accompanied investigation of the Jewishness of Jesus and the Jewish milieu of the New Testament.[9] One result has been the attention given to the Hellenistic-Jewish environment which specifies Paul's identity and determines the strategy with which he operates as a missionary in the Mediterranean world.[10]

---

[8]Richard J. Cassidy, *Society and Politics in the Acts of the Apostles* (Maryknoll, New York: Orbis, 1987) 14.

[9]In direction-setting works, the Jewishness of Paul is treated by Wayne Meeks, ed., *The Writings of St. Paul* (New York: W. W. Norton & Co., 1972), and E. P. Sanders, *Paul and Palestinian Judaism* (Philadelphia: Fortress Press, 1977); J. Christian Beker, *Paul the Apostle: The Triumph of God in Life and Thought* (Philadelphia: Fortress Press, 1980); Wayne A. Meeks, *The First Urban Christians: The Social World of the Apostle Paul* (New Haven and London: Yale University Press, 1983) 32–39. While Pauline studies in the past have tended to emphasize the Hellenistic setting of Paul's life and thought, scholarship since the late 1970s and early 1980s has given new attention to the Jewish milieu. Meeks acknowledges the tremendous variety and range within Jewish theology and among the cultural expressions of Judaism in the first-century Mediterranean world.

[10]Some Jewish scholars are also recognizing that the Christian Scriptures offer insight into the dynamics of first-century Judaism. See Alan F. Segal, *Paul the Convert: The Apostolate and Apostasy of Saul the Pharisee* (New Haven and London: Yale University Press, 1990). See also Henry J. Cad-

Another has been a wrestling with previous interpretations of Luke's treatment of Jews in his narrative. Was Luke anti-Jewish or sympathetic to Judaism and Jews?[11]

A newer reading of Acts affirms that Luke emphasized Paul's Jewishness; Paul was a man loyal to his own tradition. How, then, shall Luke's supposed antagonism toward Paul's synagogue audiences be reconciled with this reading? Luke in fact shows intimate familiarity with Jewish customs in the Gospel and throughout Acts. He offers a sympathetic presentation of Paul's religious history, and recounts continuing conversations between Paul and his co-religionists.[12] This new conviction about Luke's sympathy toward Judaism makes necessary an explanation other than Luke's "theology of displacement" to interpret the scenes involving opposition by some Jews to Paul.

When interpreted as part of the structure of a five-part type-scene in Acts 13–18, opposition from some Jews and Gentiles is

---

bury, "Acts and Eschatology," *The Background of the New Testament and Its Eschatology: In Honour of Charles Harold Dodd,* ed. William David Davies and David Daube (Cambridge: Cambridge University Press, 1956) 300–21. The latter three are reliable interpreters of the Lukan corpus within the context of New Testament theology in dialogue with its Jewish heritage. Their recognition of the importance of the Jewish milieu of the New Testament anticipated the scholarship of the 1980s.

[11]See the essays in Joseph B. Tyson, ed., *Luke-Acts and the Jewish People: Eight Critical Perspectives* (Minneapolis: Augsburg, 1988). See Tyson's recent study, *Images of Judaism in Luke-Acts* (Columbia: University of South Carolina Press, 1992). He proposes that Luke-Acts was originally an evangelistic text directed toward readers Luke regarded as God-fearers. This profile of the implied reader and audience should shape our present interpretation.

[12]David L. Tiede, *Prophecy and History in Luke-Acts* (Philadelphia: Fortress Press, 1980) 8. Luke shows great familiarity with the ritual of the synagogue. "In fact, his descriptions of synagogue ritual with detailed observations on the regular use of readings from the law and the prophets for exposition and theological disputation are still among the most complete literary accounts of first-century synagogue practice available (cf. Luke 4:16-30; Acts 13:14-43; 15:21; 17:1-4, 10-11; 18:24-26)." In Acts, the "distinction between Jew and Gentile is consistently maintained, and there is never any suggestion that somehow a 'new Israel' that includes gentile Christian believers has supplanted or displaced the Jews" (p. 10).

necessary to propel the missionary episode forward.[13] Paul—and the gospel message—thereby get thrust into a judicial setting, which involves engagement by the legal representatives of the Roman government. As a result of opposition to his preaching, Paul has to move to another location. Here, the contributions of literary analysis and form criticism press for too facile a conclusion about Luke's negative attitude toward Judaism or his ecclesial theology of displacement. Luke's focus, rather, remains on Paul—the witness and the accused—who must press forward from syngagogue to courtroom to give his testimony, ultimately before governors and kings.

Luke's overarching vision dramatizes the movement of the gospel from a religious to a secular sphere, not merely from one religious audience to another, as from synagogue to Church. The interrogation and trial scenes involving both Peter and Paul function to make clear this theological perspective. It is finally through Paul the witness that the gospel ends up addressed not only to synagogue congregations and Jewish religious leaders but to governors and kings in the secular world. The public arena of the power of Rome, epitomized in its judicial system, represents the gospel's ultimate destiny to reach "the ends of the earth." Luke's vision of the destiny of the gospel itself is most accurately the expression of his politics.

A more adequate identification of a five-stage type-scene shows that the missionary encounters from Antioch of Pisidia (13:24-52) to Corinth (18:1-17) are controlled by a repetitive compositional structure. The narrative structure guarantees a certain order of events, so that the movement of Paul's message—and the Church's preaching—is from a Jewish to a Gentile audience. However, this movement is only a piece of a larger theological trajectory in Acts, also embodied in the structure of the type-scene.

Luke-Acts, like all the writings of the New Testament, is addressed to the believing community for its own instruction and encouragement. It is not dedicated to unbelieving civil magistrates with little understanding of either Judaism or Christianity. The evangelist documents the community's history as a spiritual, di-

---

[13]See "Biblical Type-Scenes and the Uses of Convention," Robert Alter, *The Art of Biblical Narrative* (New York: Basic Books, 1981) 47-62.

vinely ordained dynamic which works itself out in the lives of individuals such as Paul. It reveals itself in the multiplication of missionary foundations and the increase of the body of believers. When the Church sees and understands itself as it truly is, it will realize its giftedness and unity. It will recognize God's benevolent action within its mysteriously unfolding history. Its pastors and teachers will take courage in present trials and maintain their hopeful orientation toward a global, missionary future. Such a future has already come to be realized in a world whose ultimate powers are not exercised within religious, but civil institutions.

If Luke re-creates Paul's biography within such a perspective, then Paul's story is to be read on two levels. First, he is the heroic apostle of the Gentiles, founder and sustainer of churches throughout the Mediterranean, and the equal of Peter. His life story as a witness is compelling because it is testimony to the power of the risen Jesus to convert the heart toward embracing a courageous new direction, no matter what trials come. As a man accused of religious and civil crimes, Paul is the patron of other beleaguered missionary teachers. The members of the Church, like Paul, may suffer accusation, trial, and imprisonment. In Luke's eyes, Paul is also the archetypal representative of the community's unfolding spiritual history of corporate conversion and communal purpose. The Spirit of God moves through the entire community like a mighty wind, charging it and empowering it for its continued mission to the ends of the earth. Ultimately, the gospel is a testimony to the resurrection of Jesus. The message is unstoppable. Resurrection means that death cannot conquer the proclamation, no matter what interrogations, trials, or opposition its preachers suffer.

1

Paul the Witness and the
Accusation Theme in Acts

Introduction

Paul assumes many roles in Acts. He is a Jew well-educated in his religious tradition and loyal to it. He is a persecutor of believers in Jesus, an investigator to be feared. Later he becomes a supporter of the community he once hunted down, and a preacher of its doctrine about Jesus. He is a person receptive to mystical experience who makes no secret of his direct communion with Jesus. Luke emphasizes his missionary activity and records his constant journeying throughout the Mediterranean to establish new communities and sustain existing ones.

One role of Paul which Luke also emphasizes is that of witness or *martyr*. In the context of the New Testament, this role is generally understood to refer to the preaching done by the apostles about Jesus. *Witness* involves a proclamation in public about belief in Jesus. Paul, like the other apostles, is a witness to Jesus because he preaches about him and calls others to faith and repentance. Paul makes public his religious motivation and convictions before people who either accept or reject him. He is not alone, but belongs to a community of believers in Jesus who all give assent to the same faith.

Besides this religious meaning of witness, Luke also uses the idea of witness in a specifically legal sense. Paul faces hearings, interrogations, trials, and judgments in a variety of religious and civil settings. From the beginning to the end of his ministry, he must deal with accusations thrown at him from many quarters. The last years of his life are consumed by the legal process, for he spends two years in prison at Caesarea, and another two under house arrest in Rome. The last eight chapters of Acts (21–28), in fact, revolve around Paul's legal status as a man accused of crimes. In telling Paul's story, Luke focuses upon scenes in which Paul makes his defense in juridical settings. Luke thus gives prominence to the legal meaning of witness when he describes Paul's impact on the history of the early Church.

Paul's role as a man accused of crimes is closely linked with the legal witness theme. By tracking Luke's use of the idea of witness, a reader acquires important information about Paul. Luke develops the meaning of witness and builds up the portrait of Paul the accused by using a number of compositional strategies. Luke uses the word *witness* in a variety of ways, and threads this vocabulary all through the narrative of Acts. He also connects the idea of witness with juridical proceedings that take place in public settings, emphasizing the secular, civil meaning of witness. Luke keeps the focus on Jerusalem as the center of activity in the early Church. Thus, most of the vocabulary about the giving of witness has a link with Jerusalem. In the last chapters of Acts, for instance, many of the accusations leveled at Paul come from his enemies based in Jerusalem. The witness theme also serves as a geographical motif, unifying the activities of Paul along the missionary circuit, especially in the cities of Miletus and Caesarea.

In developing the witness theme, Luke makes use of a literary convention, that of the *double,* to emphasize the likeness of Paul to Peter; both are evangelical witnesses. This is a particularly important aspect of the portraiture of Paul, for Luke's intention is to legitimize the missionary's authority by providing him with the same credentials as Peter, those established by being a witness to Jesus and facing the legal consequences before religious and secular judges.[1] Luke describes several legal entanglements with the Sanhedrin that Peter faces as a result of his preaching;

---

[1] See also the parallels between Jesus and Paul, and between Jesus and the disciples in Acts, outlined by Robert F. O'Toole, *The Unity of Luke's Theology: An Analysis of Luke-Acts* (Wilmington: Glazier, 1984) 62–94.

later, Paul too appears before religious authorities. However, more emphasis is given to Paul's juridical confrontations in Acts. His function as a legal witness eventually incorporates all his other roles.

I. *Witness Vocabulary Is Threaded Throughout Acts*

Witness is the one term which contributes most to developing Paul's portrait as a man accused. Luke makes strategic use of the word *witness* which occurs in a variety of contexts throughout Acts, always allowing links to be made directly or indirectly with Paul. As a noun, *witness* refers to a specific person, such as Stephen (Acts 22:20) or Paul (22:15; 26:16). It can refer to a yet-to-be-named person qualified to replace Judas as one of the Twelve (1:21), or to a group of persons such as Peter and the disciples who identify themselves as official witnesses of the resurrection (1:8; 2:32; 3:15; 5:32; 10:39; 10:41; 13:31). It also designates antagonists such as false witnesses (6:13) and those who stoned Stephen (7:58). The noun is thus highly connotative, and can refer to legal function, apostolic role or ecclesial position, religious experience, manner of death, or dramatic role.

As a modifier, *witnessed* refers to one's reputation for uprightness. Such a person's character is witnessed to by the community, e.g., the seven men who are to be chosen as deacons by the Jerusalem community (6:3). The centurion Cornelius is witnessed to by the Jews (10:22). The upright character of Timothy is verified by the believers in Lystra and Iconium (16:2). The piety of Ananias is witnessed to by other Jews (22:12).

Witness also names the content of someone's communication about God's word. For example, the apostles give witness or testimony with great power (4:33), and Paul's witness or testimony will not be received in Jerusalem (22:18). It also refers to the Tent of Meeting set up by Moses on God's instructions as the tent of witness in the Exodus wandering (7:44).

As a verb, *witness* describes what the prophets have done in anticipating the work of Jesus (10:43), what God himself does in relation to David (13:22), what God does on behalf of the disciples in affirming their mission to the Jews (14:3), what God has done in pouring out the Spirit upon the Gentiles (15:8), what God does to make his reality known to Gentiles in Lystra (14:17), and how the Holy Spirit warns Paul of coming suffering (20:23). Paul uses the verb to describe what he has done in Miletus before his congregation (20:21, 24, 26). Paul says the high priest and council of elders can witness to the trust they had in him as a messenger (22:5; 26:5). Paul himself goes on witnessing to small and great (26:22) and to Jews who come to him in Rome (28:23).

Intensive forms of *witness* appear in several places and reinforce the juridical context of witness. *Diamartyria* refers to the testimony of a witness who is appearing on behalf of someone else. In the courtroom the testimony of such a witness can be challenged by the opposing party according the procedure of *diamartyria.*[2] In Acts, the word is sometimes translated "solemnly witnessed" or "energetically witnessed." In classical usage it refers to what the witness says about one of the primary parties in a legal dispute. To validate the testimony at the same time, the witness defends his or her own worth as a giver of testimony. The intensive form of *witness* implies that in a court setting, both the primary party and the witness for the primary party are involved in the trial or hearing. *Diamartyria* implies that testimony from the supporting witnesses on behalf of a primary party is subject to legal challenge. The verifiability of the testimony itself must be proved. It is not sufficient merely to present evidence in support of someone whose case is being judged. The witnesses themselves are liable to testing and judgment.

One pattern of consistency is the intensive form of witness which appears in reference to what the disciples do. Luke uses it to describe Peter's testimony on Pentecost in Jerusalem (2:40), and again to refer to the activities of a group of disciples who are evangelizing Samaritan villages on their way back to Jerusalem (8:25). The word is placed on Peter's lips in speaking to Cornelius and his household at Caesarea when Peter says that this is what Jesus commanded the disciples to do, to *witness* to the fact that Jesus is the one chosen to be judge of the living and the dead (10:42).

Most of the uses of the intensive form of *witness,* however, are associated with Paul, a connection which underscores the juridical aspect of his evangelical witness. For instance, "solemn wit-

[2]Douglas M. MacDowell, "Diamartyria," *The Law in Classical Athens* (Ithaca: Cornell University Press, 1978) 212–19.

ness'' describes what Paul has been offering his Jewish hearers in Corinth before Silas and Timothy arrive (18:5). Paul describes his own experience in Miletus, where he says that he was witnessing to both Jews and Greeks (20:21), that the Holy Spirit gave him witness that he should expect suffering ahead (20:23), and that he wants to complete the service he has been assigned—to witness to the gospel (20:24). Luke reports that in a vision to the imprisoned Paul, Jesus says, ''Have courage. As you did witness to the things about me in Jerusalem, so it is necessary to witness in Rome'' (23:11). Finally, Luke uses the intensive form to describe Paul's witness to great numbers of Jews in Rome (28:23).

Of the thirty-nine instances of *witness* vocabulary in Acts, most occur in passages in which Luke assigns the lines to major actors in the narrative. Jesus speaks to the disciples before his Ascension (1:8), and addresses Paul in a vision (22:18; 23:11; 26:16). Peter uses witness terminology in his various sermons and addresses.[3] Others who speak at significant moments in Acts include Stephen in his sermon (7:44), the messengers of Cornelius who come to bring Peter to Caesarea (10:22), and Ananias who exhorts Paul (22:15). Paul himself uses more witness terminology than anyone else.[4] Among all the designated narrators, it is clear that the use of witness vocabulary is concentrated on the lips of Peter (eleven times) and of Paul (twelve times).

While the role of witness is assigned by Luke to both Peter and Paul, there are three episodes in particular which emphasize witness vocabulary. The Cornelius-Peter encounter employs witness vocabulary five times (Acts 10:22, 39, 41, 42, 43). In Paul's farewell address at Miletus (20:18-35) there are four uses. In Paul's Jerusalem speech (Acts 22:1-22), witness vocabulary occurs five times. Peter is the speaker in the Cornelius-Peter encounter, but Paul dominates the speeches at Miletus and Jerusalem. Thus, in these three episodes, Luke shifts the weight of witness to Paul's side.[5]

[3]Peter's use of witness vocabulary occurs in Acts 1:22; 2:32, 40; 3:15; 5:32; 6:3; 10:39, 41, 42, 43; 15:8.

[4]Paul's use of witness language: Acts 13:22; 13:31; 14:17; 20:21, 23, 24, 26; 22:5, 12, 20; 26:5, 22.

[5]In contrast to the thirty cases where characters within Acts are designated as narrators, there are nine instances where the speaking voice is that

II. Witness in Public and the Civil Meaning of Witness

It is evident that witness vocabulary is typically connected with activity in the public forum, for confrontational scenes in Acts usually take place within view and hearing of a city's populace in Acts. The words of Luke's main speakers are thus capable of being heard and attested to by an audience. Such scenes include Peter's sermons in Jerusalem (Acts 2:14-36; 3:12-26) and Stephen's trial before the Sanhedrin (7:2-54). Other confrontations that involve public audiences include the disciples' response to their judges (5:29-32), Paul's farewell to the Miletus congregation when he says that the Holy Spirit has warned him about coming suffering (20:23), Paul's defense before a mob in Jerusalem (22:1-21), and his hearing at Caesarea before a governor, king, and court guests (26:1-23).

Luke, like a great film producer, works with many "extras." He narrates events and reproduces dialogue in such a way that significant scenes are peopled with onlookers, reporters, co-actors, and co-narrators. Luke reports occasions which either sympathetic or unsympathetic participants could verify. This socialization of the texts seems intentional rather than accidental as a narrative strategy, just as any dramatist chooses how many characters will occupy the stage at any one time. Luke also gradually widens the circle of who constitutes the "public" in Acts. At the beginning of Acts, when events are centered in Jerusalem, the public is predominantly Jewish. In the middle of Acts, during the missionary journeys of Paul, the public is a mix of Jewish and Gentile hearers. In the last six chapters, Paul's public includes Jewish and Gentile hearers, but it has become predominantly Gentile in the persons of Roman political and military officials. Be they sympathetic or unsympathetic to Paul, be they witnesses for the prosecution or for his defense, the participants themselves become witnesses to the testimony of Paul about his life story. There is,

---

of the Lukan narrator, with witness activity referring to Peter's exhortation of the crowd at Pentecost (2:40), the apostles' preaching (4:33; 8:25), the false witnesses responsible for Stephen's legal condemnation (6:13) and Stephen's death by stoning (7:58), God's affirmation of the message of Paul and Barnabas (14:3), Timothy's character attested to by the Christians in Lystra and Iconium (16:2), and Paul's preaching (18:5; 28:23).

ultimately, no privatized religious experience in Acts. Any interior, private disclosures eventually are proclaimed to a community. In becoming a matter of public record, these disclosures are available for either the scrutiny or the edification of others. As Paul maintains concerning his entire ministry, "This was not done in a corner" (26:26).

The witness vocabulary in Acts reinforces a pattern of compositional preference in the book. What Luke emphasizes in the story of the Church's growth is not the mystical, transformative, and personal character of the Christian movement, but its public, verifiable, and participative dimension. The personal is incorporated into the public, not the public into the personal.

III. Those Who Witness Are Linked to Jerusalem

Another general observation about witness vocabulary in Acts is its association with Jerusalem. In an important speech of Paul's (22:1-22), this concentration on Jerusalem provides an orienting principle for his autobiographical review. Paul says he was raised in the city, educated there, and was a witness to Stephen's death there. From Jerusalem, he was sent out by religious leaders to bring back to the city heretics he would arrest in Damascus. On another occasion, when he visited Jerusalem after his conversion, he had a vision in the Temple. At the end of his missionary journeys, he returned to Jerusalem on Pentecost. There he was arrested and defended himself before the crowd and later the Sanhedrin.

Jesus' final words to the disciples are spoken in Jerusalem: "You are to be my witnesses in Jerusalem, throughout Judea and Samaria, even to the ends of the earth" (1:8). Peter calls for the election of a new disciple and addresses the community in Jerusalem (1:21). Peter preaches to the crowds in Jerusalem on Pentecost, identifying the Eleven as witnesses (2:32, 40). After curing the lame man who used to sit at the Beautiful Gate of the Temple, Peter addresses the Jews from Solomon's Portico at the Temple (3:15).

In the context of describing the primitive community of Jerusalem, Luke reviews the testimony the apostles were giving to the resurrection (4:33). Peter and the other apostles give answer to the high priest and council in Jerusalem after defying their order not to preach (5:32). The Twelve address the Jerusalem community and call on the congregation to choose seven men as deacons who have a good reputation (6:3). The incident of Stephen's arrest takes place in Jerusalem. False witnesses claim that Stephen has spoken against the holy place, the Temple in Jerusalem (6:13). Stephen's reference to the Tent of Meeting is made in a speech to the chief priest and elders in Jerusalem (7:44). In the account of Stephen's death at Jerusalem, the ones who stone him are called witnesses (7:58). Thus, a variety of speakers who use witness vocabulary are all located in Jerusalem. When Paul adopts the same language later in Acts, a precedent has been set associating him with the apostolic spokespersons earlier in the narrative. Luke creates a pattern of association between the meaning of witness and the centrality of the Church's activity, grafting Paul into the continuum.

Luke reinforces the character of Paul as a witness by linking this role with the apostolic missionary enterprise which originated in Jerusalem. He narrates the going out of the missionary disciples beyond Jerusalem and their return: " . . . having witnessed and having spoken the word of the Lord, they returned to Jerusalem and evangelized many villages of the Samaritans" (8:25). Peter says to Cornelius and his household in Caesarea, "We are witnesses to all that he did in the land of the Jews and in Jerusalem" (10:39). Paul, preaching at the synagogue in Antioch in Pisidia, refers to the resurrection of Jesus in Jerusalem: "Yet God raised him from the dead, who for many days appeared to the ones who came up with him from Galilee to Jerusalem who now are his witnesses before the people" (13:31). Peter addresses the Church in Jerusalem and validates the Gentile mission by defending God's witness to the Gentiles and their reception of the Holy Spirit (15:8).

In Jerusalem, Paul reports his previous connection with the high priest and whole council of elders who had given him letters in Jerusalem to take to Jews in Damascus (22:5). Paul tells the crowd about a vision of Jesus he had had in Jerusalem, and his admission to Jesus that, years before, he had been present at the death of Stephen who was killed in Jerusalem (22:20). Paul shares with the Jerusalem crowd his vision of Jesus in the Temple when Jesus said to him, "Hurry and go forth quickly out of Jerusalem because they will not receive your witness concerning me" (22:18). While Paul is imprisoned but under the protective custody of Roman soldiers in Jerusalem, Jesus appears to him in vision and says, "As you witnessed those things concerning me in Jerusalem, so it is necessary to witness in Rome" (23:11). Paul, speaking before Agrippa and Festus in Caesarea, tells of his seizure by the Jews in Jerusalem at the Temple court as the immediate prelude to his insistence that "I stand here witnessing to small and to great . . . " (26:22). Thus, the Church's apostolic mission throughout the Mediterranean is summarized by a review of the occasions when witness vocabulary is used. Paul proves to be an especially visible witness because of his speeches made as a defendant while he is under arrest.

Luke plays out the witness theme by capitalizing on both the tension and the succession of Paul's confrontations with religious and civil interrogators. The tension with religious leaders over theological issues is highlighted by the association of witness with the Temple in Jerusalem. The Temple itself is a vital part of the backdrop several times in connection with *witness*. For example, Peter addresses the crowd from Solomon's Portico (3:15). The accusers of Stephen say he has spoken against the holy place which is the Temple (6:13). Paul remembers his vision of Jesus in the Temple (22:18, 20). He also reviews with Agrippa the trauma he experienced when the Jews arrested him in the Temple court and tried to kill him (26:22).

Representing the opposition of religious authorities to the apostles' preaching, the dramatic role of the Sanhedrin reinforces the association between Jerusalem and the witness passages. The apostles give witness after returning from a second appearance before the Sanhedrin (4:33). Peter and the other apostles give answer to the high priest before the Sanhedrin (5:29-32). Those who arrest Stephen lead him off to the Sanhedrin (6:12-13). Paul speaks of his association with the high priest and council of elders in his former days (22:5).

Luke's intentional link between the witness theme and Jerusalem is indicated by the frequency of the association. Jerusalem is named at least sixty times in Acts. In twenty of the thirty-nine uses of witness vocabulary, Jerusalem is mentioned or is the actual location of the event being narrated by Luke. Jerusalem is often the speaker's location, or the place to which the speaker refers. This sort of repetition serves to support a thematic association between *witness* and *Jerusalem* that weaves its way throughout the narrative of Acts. Even though episodes may be chronologically and geographically separated from one another, the relation between *witness* and *Jerusalem* remains strong.

IV. Theme of Witness and the Missionary Circuit

Besides Jerusalem, where else does Luke locate persons who give witness? The word *witness* is associated, in addition to Jerusalem, with two principal locations, Caesarea Maritima and Miletus. Caesarea provides a link with *witness* seven times where it is the scene of Peter's witness to Cornelius (10:39, 41, 42, 43) and the scene of Paul's speech to Agrippa and Festus (26:5, 16, 22). At Miletus, on the eve of Paul's journey to Jerusalem, four instances of witness vocabulary occur in Paul's farewell to the Ephesian elders and the community (20:21, 23, 24, 26).[6]

What is striking is the spatial concreteness which grounds witness vocabulary. Temporal markers for events, by contrast, may be less exact. The sequence of Paul's biography, which he recounts during his defense before the crowd in Jerusalem (Acts 22:1-22), is closely tied to specific persons rather than exact times. Paul thus speaks of his education with Gamaliel, his mandate to go to Damascus received from the high priest, the vision in which Jesus spoke to him, and his healing from blindness by Ananias. He is never very precise about year or month, and the chronol-

---

[6]In addition to Jerusalem, Caesarea, and Miletus, the witness vocabulary is linked with places evangelized by the disciples on their missionary journeys: when Samaritan villages receive the witness of the disciples (8:25); when Paul gives a speech in the synagogue at Antioch in Pisidia (13:22, 31) ; when Paul and Barnabas are preaching in Iconium to both believing and unbelieving Jews and Gentiles (14:3); in Lystra by Paul and Barnabas protesting to the priest of Zeus and Gentile citizens (14:17); to describe what Paul is doing in Corinth with Jews before Silas and Timothy arrive (18:5); in the context of reporting Paul's Damascus conversion experience (22:5, 12; 26:16); in reference to Rome (23:11; 28:33).

ogy about which Luke is rather vague preoccupies later historical critics.[7]

Instead of giving a specific time, Luke ties events to geographical locations such as Jerusalem, Damascus, Joppa, Caesarea,
Macedonia, Corinth, Lystra, Miletus, and Rome. Thus, the witness theme is given concreteness and historicity by geographical
allusion rather than a calendar's exactitude. Luke attaches significance not merely to witness as a theological idea, but to that
witness given in the specific places where Paul preached, where
he was accused, and where he defended himself.

V. Peter and Paul as Witnesses to Jesus

Luke's portrait of Paul as an accused witness is built up by various narrational techniques. One of Luke's strategies is called *doubling,* by which he reminds readers of the likeness between two
persons. In Acts, for instance, the healings accomplished by Peter
and Paul replicate those of Jesus. Thus, the acts of Peter and Paul
continue to manifest the power of the living Jesus.

Within Acts, the technique of doubling also establishes a har-
monious relationship between Peter and Paul. Several advantages
for Paul result. His actions match those of Peter. As Peter's
sufferings mirror those of Jesus, so Paul's mission is a continua-
tion of the work of Jesus. Paul's mission is legitimated within
the Church on two counts: he is like Jesus and he is like Peter.
If Paul resembles Jesus and Peter, then Paul's leadership and his
convictions as a missionary have validity. The narrative strategy
of doubling serves Luke's theological and pastoral purposes as
they are personified in Paul.

The evangelist expended considerable effort as a literary artist
in pursuing the goal of legitimizing Paul. One of the principal
ways Luke develops the doubling of Peter and Paul is through
their role as witnesses. They are both witnesses to the resurrection and they are both witnesses and preachers of the gospel.
Proclaiming the story of Jesus, they are witnesses to the Gentiles.

[7]See Gerd Lüdemann, *Paul, Apostle to the Gentiles: Studies in Chronology* (Philadelphia: Fortress Press, 1984).

The mission of Peter and Paul is reinforced by what they have seen and heard in visions which have re-oriented their activities. Lastly, they are witnesses who have been destined and chosen beforehand by God.

a. Witnesses to the Resurrection

> You will receive power when the Holy Spirit comes down on you; then you are to be my witnesses in Jerusalem, throughout Judea and Samaria, yes, even to the ends of the earth (Acts 1:8).

From the beginning of Acts, the role of witness is Peter's, but thematically includes Paul. Jesus speaks to "the apostles he had chosen through the Holy Spirit," implying the Twelve. But the prior narration in Luke's Gospel indicates that Jesus manifested himself in appearances, gave instruction, and showed he was alive to many more than the Twelve. Such witnesses include the women (Luke 24:1-10), the disciples at Emmaus (Luke 24:13-32), and those assembled with the Eleven who hear the report of the Emmaus pair and witness the appearance of Jesus (Luke 24:33). It would seem that Luke uses the term *apostle* inclusively rather than exclusively in Acts. *Apostles* refers generally in Acts to a large company, not just the Twelve. The relation established between "the apostles" and Paul by the witness theme implies that Paul has equivalence with the Twelve. *Apostle* is for Luke an inclusive description, as is *witness*.[8] Luke's preferred description for naming the followers of Jesus is *witness,* not *apostle* or "one of the Twelve."

Jesus sends his followers to be witnesses to the ends of the earth. The mandate applies to many others besides the Eleven gathered at the Ascension. If Paul's missionary journeys take him to the

---

[8]Beverly R. Gaventa, *From Darkness to Light: Aspects of Conversion in the New Testament* (Philadelphia: Fortress Press, 1986) 84: "Luke employs the term 'witness' to describe the work of the apostles. Prior to his ascension Jesus tells them that they will be witnesses (Luke 24:48, Acts 1:8), and Luke regularly characterizes them as such (Acts 1:22; 2:32; 3:15; 5:32; 10:39, 41; 13:31). For Paul to be called a witness (cf. 22:15) is for his work to be considered the same as that of the Twelve, even though he cannot properly be called an apostle."

ends of the earth, then he too must be a witness commissioned by the original mandate of Jesus. In Paul's case, "ends of the earth" means both furthest geographic extent and highest political power. Later, Jesus refers to Paul's activity, not by reviewing the witness that he gave all over the Mediterranean area and throughout Asia, but by referring to his witness in Jerusalem: "Make haste and get quickly out of Jerusalem" (Acts 22:18). The haste was made necessary precisely by a series of activities which had inflamed the Jerusalemites. The preaching of Paul had aroused the hostility of his hearers (9:28-29). So did his defense speech before the mob (22:1-22) and his subsequent Sanhedrin hearing (23:1-10). All the testimony of Paul is encapsulated within the witness given in Jerusalem: "As you have witnessed to the matters concerning me in Jerusalem, so must you do in Rome" (23:11).

While Peter defines the period from the baptism of John to the ascension as the duration qualifying someone to be a witness, the role derives its existence from the fact of Jesus' resurrection. A follower of Jesus witnesses to an event. "It is entirely fitting therefore, that one of those who was of our company while the Lord Jesus moved among us, from the baptism of John until the day he was taken up from us, should be named as witness with us to his resurrection" (Acts 1:21). Being named as witness does not change a person's experience, or endow the follower of Jesus with new expertise. To be named a witness means that the follower's previous experience of the historical Jesus is now to be shared with others. In its formal expression, this sharing is officially recognized both as an ecclesial responsibility and as a formal role in the community of faith. In this understanding of witness, Paul qualifies, with Peter and "our company," as a witness to the resurrection.

b. *Witnesses and Preachers*

One of the roles of the witness is to preach publicly before an assembled crowd. The first chapters of Acts present Peter as a witness whose preaching stirs his audiences and evokes their conversion. The prosecutorial tone of Peter (3:19) is consistent with his exhortations in the first part of Acts. The role allows him to take a vigorous stance while accusing his audience and calling for their repentance. It is a successful forensic posture, expressing the position of power Peter occupies and the authoritativeness of his theological conviction. His style of communication, reminiscent of the prophets who exhorted their own communities in a similar tone, produces mass conversions in Jerusalem.

Later in Acts, Paul is less successful when he operates from this stance. In fact, Paul's authoritative posture antagonizes his hearers instead of inspiring their repentance. In the sermons and legal encounters of Peter in the first five chapters of Acts, the accusations brought against the disciples are defended on the same grounds that the disciples might use to defend Jesus himself. Peter maintains both ideological and legal control of the situations which confront him. He calls his hearers to a change of view even before they can debate him. By contrast, the last third of Acts shows Paul accused of wrongdoing and losing control of the situation rather than becoming its master. Paul is reduced to a defensive, explanatory role, with his responses controlled by the accusations piled up against him by his opponents.

c. *Initiators of the Mission to the Gentiles*

Luke tightens the relationship between Peter and Paul by describing both of them as initiators of the outreach to the Gentiles. It may generally be thought that Paul was the originator, but Luke's retelling of the history of the Church gives Peter as well as Paul a claim to this leadership position. Luke legitimates Paul's mission to the Gentiles by showing that it was mandated by the Church at large. But as Luke retells the story, Peter's outreach to the Gentiles begins earlier when he answers the summons God addresses to Cornelius (Acts 10:4). Before the whole assembly, Peter justifies the inclusion of the Gentiles within the community of believers (11:1-18). He affirms that God has given the same gift of the Spirit to the Gentiles as to the original Jewish community (11:17)

The call Luke assigns to Peter in Acts is not that which Paul describes in his own letter to the Galatians. There, Paul identifies the uncircumcised Gentiles as his special mission, while Peter preaches to the Jews. Paul calls Peter to account for requiring the Gentiles to adopt Jewish customs (Gal 2:1-14). In Acts, by contrast, Luke makes Peter the spokesperson for the inclusion of Gentiles in the community and the one to make official the liberation of the Gentiles from the requirement of circumcision.[9] This shift in roles and positions may underline the Lukan effort to legitimize the Pauline mission by having it "originate" with recognized hierarchical authority.

Paul's mission to the Gentiles, according to the Lukan perspective, did not originate with Paul, but with the movement of God within the Church in diverse and complex ways. One important instance was the contact of Peter with Cornelius. At the same time, missionary work to the Gentiles was simultaneously arising in Antioch (Acts 11:20-21). The development was approved by Barnabas who visited Antioch as a delegate from the Church in Jerusalem (11:22-24). Paul's mission is placed within this larger context of the outreach of the whole Church to the Gentiles. This ecclesial direction did not entail an abandonment of its preaching in the synagogues, but was an expansion to include Gentiles with whom conversation arose. Antioch was one location where Gentiles were receptive to preaching about Jesus. Other Gentiles actually initiated this encounter and invited a conversation with Jewish preachers (e.g., Cornelius).

d. Receivers of Inaugural Visions

A fourth link between Paul and Peter lies in their reception of inaugural visions which reorient and clarify the mission of each witness. Peter has a midday vision on the rooftop at Joppa which resolves his hesitancy about eating with Gentiles (10:9-16). The visions of Cornelius and Peter are so interlocked that the testi-

[9]See Paul J. Achtemeier, *The Quest for Unity in the New Testament Church: A Study in Paul and Acts* (Philadelphia: Fortress Press, 1987). He discusses the split in the Gentile mission resulting from conflict between Barnabas and Paul over Mark (Acts 15:36-41). Achtemeier regards this argument over John Mark a Lukan "cover" for the much deeper split in missionary policy toward Gentile converts. This disjunction is implied by lack of reference to circumcision both in Acts 11:1-18, and in the decrees at the Council at Jerusalem (15:6-21). From Paul's letters, it would appear that the circumcision issue was prominent as a pastoral issue in his missionary endeavors.

mony of each man corroborates and is completed by the testimony of the other. The message Cornelius is intended to hear cannot be completed until his vision is reported to Peter; and Peter's vision cannot be interpreted until he has spoken with Cornelius. The process of interaction between separate but coordinate testimonies is set in motion by messengers from Cornelius. His obedience to the vision's directive attests to its reality (10:22-23).

In the same way, a complex structure of coordinating testimony underlies the vision of Ananias and the vision of Saul (9:3-19). In Damascus where Saul is waiting, still blinded, he has a vision of Ananias coming to him. At the same time, Ananias is having a vision of the Lord telling him to go to Saul. When joined, the religious experience of each man validates the other's vision. The testimony of two witnesses to God's intervention is given (9:17-19). Ananias, an independent witness, provides validation of Saul's experience by acknowledging that Jesus appeared to Saul on the way to Damascus. He knows that Saul was blinded by the vision (9:17). Saul's vision of Ananias anticipates his coming. Like Peter's validation by the Spirit (10:19), Saul's vision of Ananias assures him that what will take place is reliable and trustworthy.[10]

Luke leaves some ambiguity about whose vision should be considered the primary catalyst for the mission to the Gentiles. Within the narrative sequence of Acts, Saul's reorienting vision (9:1-18) occurs before Peter's (10:9-16). Nevertheless, Peter's vision actually generates a change in policy toward the Gentiles. The admission of Cornelius and his household into the Church establishes a precedent for Paul's later missionary activity. However, Paul, rather than Peter, is the one whose mission to the Gentiles is eventually given the most importance in Acts. Luke devotes the last half of Acts to the story of Paul's own missionary adventures by land and by sea, and in outreach to both Jews and Gentiles.

---

[10]See the discussion of the Lukan technique of doubling visions in the Gospel and Acts by Michael D. Goulder, *Luke: A New Paradigm,* Journal for the Study of the New Testament Supplement Series 20 (Sheffield: Sheffield Academic Press, 1989) 1:205-06.

e. Witnesses Destined Beforehand by God

When Peter addresses the household of Cornelius, he describes the role of those who testify to Jesus as foreordained: " . . . witnesses as had been chosen beforehand by God, who ate and drank with him after he rose from the dead" (10:41). At what particular time God made such a choice of witnesses is not clear. Peter's assertion refers to some moment in salvation history in which certain followers were destined, like prophets, to do this particular sacred task.[11]

It is to this origin because of God's destined choice that Ananias refers when he affirms Paul's role as a witness: "The God of our fathers long ago designated you to know his will, to look upon the Just One and to hear the sound of his voice. Before all people you are to be his witness to what you have seen and heard" (22:15). In the Lukan perspective, seeing and hearing are equivalent to "eating and drinking with him after he rose from the dead." Paul fulfills the most basic requirements for giving testimony to Jesus. God chose Paul. Paul saw Jesus and he heard Jesus speaking to him. For Luke, the roles of prophet and witness are merged, and Paul incarnates both.

At the beginning of Acts, there are several terms for the followers of Jesus: *apostles, disciples, brothers,* and *witnesses.* Gradually, the terms of *apostle* (Acts 16:4 is the last use) and *disciple* (Acts 21:16 is the last use) drop away. Only the term *witness* is carried through the beginning, middle, and end of Acts. In Luke's view, Paul's status as a witness makes him the equivalent of an apostle. Being a witness is the most fundamental meaning of apostleship, according to Luke.

f. Juridical Appearances of Peter Anticipate Those of Paul

Luke often emphasizes a specifically legal context for witness vocabulary in Acts. He is concerned to build up the portrait of Paul as a man accused of various crimes. The doubling of Peter and Paul reinforces the role they share in common as witness in

---

[11]Prophets speak of their sense of destiny and of their intuition that they are following a course already appointed for them by God. See Isaiah 44:2; 49:1; Jeremiah 1:4-5.

a legal sense. Early in Acts, Luke dramatizes Peter's appearances before the religious court in Jerusalem. These anticipate the trial scenes of Paul later in the narrative, when his credibility as a witness gains strength from the precedent that Peter has already provided.

The confrontation of Peter and John by the Sanhedrin had ended with the religious leaders' unenforceable command: not to speak or teach in the name of Jesus (4:18). Peter and John countered this judgment with one of their own. They called on the judges themselves to decide whether it was right to be obedient to them rather than to God. "For we cannot but speak the things which we have seen and heard" (4:19). The disciples gave witness in great power (4:33) by continuing to give direct, experiential testimony to the person called Jesus. They chose to follow their own judgment concerning what was just (*dikaion,* 4:19). They thus separated themselves from submission to the Sanhedrin.[12]

It is perhaps not by chance that Luke includes in the narration of Paul's conversion an allusion to the justice or innocence of Jesus, who also was once arraigned before a religious tribunal. Just as Peter gives an account of his actions—first to the Jewish crowd in the Temple area, and later to the Sanhedrin (5:27-33)—so does Paul first give an account of himself to the Jewish crowd in the Temple area (22:1-21), and later to the Sanhedrin (23:1-7). Ananias affirms Paul's mission, saying, "The God of our fathers appointed you . . . to see the Just One and to hear a voice from his mouth" (22:14). Ananias continues, "For you will be a witness for him to all men of what you have seen and heard" (22:15). The one to whom Paul will give witness is the Just One (22:14) whom he has seen and whose voice he has heard. Paul's witness is judged according to legal standards. He is qualified to give testimony because he has seen Jesus personally and heard him directly.

What are some of Luke's purposes for presenting Peter and Paul in juridical settings? Juridical confrontation provides verification of the defendants' testimony. Legal judgments and discipli-

---

[12]See Paul Ramsey, "The Biblical Norm of Righteousness," *Interpretation* 24 (1979) 419-29.

nary action prove that juridical procedures cannot alter what the defendants have seen and heard. An interrogation before the Sanhedrin does not leave the judges with satisfactory answers other than the disciples' own explanation for events. The continuing witness of the disciples implies that their maintaining the facts about Jesus may target them repeatedly for legal action. However, the believers' experience of the "great power" can neither be subsumed under the categories provided by the juridical setting nor lose its force. Luke suggests than an order to stop preaching, given by the Sanhedrin, cannot put limits on God's power. God's power transcends the control religious or civil authorities might attempt to establish over the disciples who exercise that power. At the same time, though, believers can be arrested and must surrender to the public process of interrogation.

During his second juridical appearance before the Sanhedrin, Peter gives answer to the High Priest in a statement that concludes with his reasons for disobeying the order to cease speaking about Jesus. "And we are witnesses of these things, and the Holy Spirit, whom God gave to those obeying him" (Acts 5:32). This interrogation takes place after the arrest and jailing of the apostles (5:18) and their miraculous deliverance by an angel (5:19). After they obey the angel's command to continue preaching in the Temple area, they are arrested again (5:26). The second interrogation continues the dialogue begun in the first trial (4:5-21).

The interrogators in the second trial are no longer concerned with identifying the source of the power by which the lame man was healed. Rather, the focus now turns to two issues: the disobedience of Peter and John, who had continued their preaching in Jerusalem, and their alleged intention to assign to the Sanhedrin responsibility for Jesus' death. "You intend to bring this man's blood upon us" (5:28). Peter's response, "We must obey God rather than men," echoes his words from the first interrogation (5:29; 4:19). Previously, an exhortation which Peter addressed to the crowd (3:12-26) had brought about a believing response from thousands of his hearers (4:4). Peter had once excused leaders because of their ignorance (3:17). The leaders do not receive Peter's challenge as an invitation, but as an accusation. Peter buttresses his testimony by saying that the "we" who are witnesses are joined by the Holy Spirit, who is also a witness, on the side of those who obey God. The obedience the apostles give to God is presented as their defense for the third time (4:19; 5:29, 32). If they are disobedient to the Sanhedrin they are nevertheless obedient to God.

A similar preoccupation with disobedience and submission runs through the Jerusalem speech of Paul (22:1-22), but from a somewhat different angle. In the Pauline speech a case is made not only for Paul's history of submission to Jewish religious authority and tradition, but for his obedience to heavenly authority as well. The defense itself provides an echo of the accusations previously brought against Paul: he was, in the eyes of his detractors, an unfaithful Jew and a violator of Jewish tradition. Luke is thus concerned to present Paul's association with Jewish leadership and his submission to it, as signs that he was truly Jewish and that his orthodoxy was respected by Jewish authorities.

Conclusion

An overview of Acts indicates that Luke takes seriously Paul's reputation as a man accused of wrongdoing, in spite of his record as a great missionary. One of Luke's purposes in Acts is to defend Paul, present his missionary activity in a truthful light, and offer him to the community as its model. This purpose is communicated partly through Luke's marked use of *witness* vocabulary in Acts. A juridical meaning of *witness* is a principal indicator that Luke is attending to the accusations against Paul.

The word *witness* appears in many geographical contexts in Acts, and Luke underlines its juridical meaning. Preaching the gospel and giving testimony in court are often synonymous public activities. Thus, *witness* is a role which encompasses both expressions of evangelization. Most instances of the vocabulary of *witness* occur in speeches by Peter and Paul. However, the scenes in which Paul uses *witness* are more numerous than Peter's. Luke links Peter and Paul, but gives emphasis to Paul's use of *witness* language.

Luke builds up the portrait of Paul the witness through various strategies besides the use of language. The act of giving witness, in sermon and in juridical testimony, is typically linked with Jerusalem. Because the center of the early Church's authority lies in Jerusalem, Paul's witness is closely tied to the Church. The location of Jerusalem serves to link Paul both to Judaism and to the original experience of the early Church. Luke wants to recognize Paul's loyalty to his Jewish tradition, as well as to validate him as a witness to the apostolic tradition of the Church.

Luke relies on the compositional device of *doubling* to feature the parallels between Peter and Paul, and the category of *witness* summarizes many of them. Both are witnesses to the resurrection of Jesus. Both are preachers of the gospel. Both can claim to be originators of the mission to the Gentiles. Both receive mysterious visions which re-orient their energies, and they claim that God has chosen them for their apostolic task. Finally, both Peter and Paul act as witnesses in juridical settings. Luke thus legitimates Paul's apostolic role and mission by his replication of Peter's witness.

2

Accusations Against Paul
Prior to the Council of Jerusalem

Introduction

Where do the accusations against Paul originate? The interrogation scenes and trials in the last third of Acts are actually the culmination of a long history of accusation endured by Paul. Luke's portrait of Paul is consistent from the beginning. From Paul's first appearance as the young man Saul, his characterization provokes contradictory responses. Loved by some, he is hated by others. There are several scenes in the first half of Acts, prior to the Council in Jerusalem, in which Luke acknowledges the basis for the accusations against the missionary. They include the death of Stephen (6:8-8:1), Paul's Damascus experience and his return to Jerusalem (9:1-30), Paul's sermon and difficulties at Antioch in Pisida (13:14-52), the episode at Iconium (14:1-6) and the incident at Lystra (14:8-23).

Luke's purpose in retelling Paul's story involves a defense of the apostle through a recontextualization of his story. Luke outlines and reconstructs the complexity of religious, social, and civil dynamics which had a negative impact on Paul's exercise of his ministry. He reviews the missionary journeys of Paul throughout the Mediterranean area. The pattern inaugurated at Antioch, Iconium, and Lystra holds true for the rest of the cities Paul visits in Acts 14-18. Luke's narrative intentionally structures these visits according to a pattern of opposition to Paul arising from various religious and secular quarters. The apostle's confrontation with both religious and secular leaders proves to be a predictable and inevitable part of his missionary activity. Accusation functions as a vehicle for driving the missionary from one city to another.[1]

At the same time, it is evident that Paul's witness moves from a synagogue audience to a non-Jewish audience and then to a civic audience. Once Paul's message engages persons outside the religious setting and in the civilian population, he then typically confronts some kind of juridical proceeding launched against him. Whether semiofficial or official, the legal process acts as a catalyst to drive Paul from the city. The process repeats itself throughout Paul's career. This pattern reinforces Luke's portrayal of Paul as a missionary vulnerable to all sorts of accusations, yet one whose mission is unstoppable.

From this perspective, Luke is more concerned with Paul than with the responses of his audiences. Both Jews and Gentiles accept Paul's message at various times, and representatives of both groups resist him. By following Paul's fortunes, Luke describes the gospel's trajectory which moves of necessity from a religious to a secular and civil arena. When Paul stands before civil magistrates defending himself against accusations or suffering their consequences, the gospel has been translated from a religious to a secular audience. Paul's interrogations and trials before civilian authorities make clear that his preaching has crossed beyond the boundary separating religious and secular worlds.

---

[1] "Despite the increased complexity, the pattern of initial acceptance followed by rejection is clearly present in Acts, both in several individual sections and in the book as a whole. . . . It is a virtual formula: Paul enters a city and preaches or teaches in a synagogue. At first there is a positive response, but later the unconverted Jews turn the masses against Paul, and he then goes out to address Gentiles. Sometimes Jews stir up non-Jews, and as a result Paul is forced to go on to another city, leaving a believing group behind. The pattern appears to be Luke's major means of shaping his narratives about Paul's activity in Pisidian Antioch (Acts 13:13-52), Iconium (14:1-7), Thessalonica (17:1-9), Beroea (17:10-15), and Ephesus (19:8-10)." See Joseph B. Tyson, *The Death of Jesus in Luke-Acts* (Columbia: University of South Carolina Press) 38-39.

I. The Presence of Saul and the Death of Stephen (Acts 6:8–8:1)

Paul makes his first appearance in Acts as the young man Saul, bystander at Stephen's death (7:58). While it casts Paul in a negative light as a collaborator with the killers of Stephen, the introduction serves several of Luke's purposes. First, Paul originally was accepted by a powerful faction of the Jewish community in Jerusalem. This acceptance meant he was regarded as religiously observant, not a maverick or heretic. Also indicated is his long-standing presence in Jerusalem at an early and crucial stage of the church's development. It is unlikely that a group of Jewish men would leave their cloaks with a stranger or someone they did not know was trustworthy. Paul is made a witness to the death of a witness to Jesus. He hears the words of Stephen and sees his actual moment of death. Luke has correlated the death of Stephen with the death of Jesus, for both pray for their persecutors (Luke 23:34; Acts 7:60) and both commend their spirits to God (Luke 23:46; Acts 7:59).

Stephen's accusers provide some clues about the identity of those who later oppose Paul. The accusers of Stephen claim he has blasphemed against Moses and God (6:11). These opponents are Jewish freedmen from the provincial areas of Cyrene, Alexandria, Cilicia, and Asia, and are emigrés to Jerusalem. It is not clear what religious or political alliance was represented by the Hellenists opposed to Stephen. They were probably religious conservatives from the diaspora, some of them from Paul's own province, the location of his birth-city, Tarsus. They seem to have been theologically aligned with the Jewish leadership in Jerusalem, at least during the episode of Stephen's death. When Stephen minimized instead of emphasized the centrality of the Temple as the center of worship, he angered these particular Hellenists, who joined forces with the Sanhedrin. Later, Jews from the same area of Asia emerge in the narrative of Acts as opponents of Paul (21:27; perhaps 14:19-20; 20:23 and 23:12; 25:19). The hostility of these particular Jews in Jerusalem to Paul may have been fed by a class difference between their freedman status and Paul's Roman citizenship (16:37-38; 22:25-28).[2]

---

[2]On the question of the Hellenists' identity, and the possible religious and

Originally, Stephen's death was probably a mob lynching. However, the confrontation between Stephen and his accusers is narrated as a formal hearing, with prosecution and defense standing before the Sanhedrin. The high priest poses the question to Stephen the defendant, just as the high priest had begun the interrogation of Peter and John at their second Sanhedrin trial (6:28). A key accusation against Stephen is that he spoke against the Temple and the Law. This is similar to the accusation circulated against Paul. James warns Paul about it (21:20-21) and Paul defends himself against it when facing Jewish accusers from Jerusalem before Festus in Caesarea (25:8). Paul, too, is accused of speaking against the Temple.

The discourse of Stephen, not surprisingly, and with more provocation than Peter's defense, meets with hostile rejection (7:54). It is a hostility similar to that Peter and John faced at their second Sanhedrin appearance (5:33). Later, Paul will meet the same hostile response from the crowd in Jerusalem (22:2-23). Thus, thematic parallels of interrogation and rejection link Paul with Peter and Stephen.

The witnesses who stone Stephen are identified with the false witnesses who brought accusations against him (6:13). The Sanhedrin hears the testimony of false witnesses. The witnesses carry out the execution of Stephen in the spirit of a lynching. "And they cast him out of the city and stoned him. And the witnesses laid down their garments at the feet of a young man called Saul" (7:58). A similar action was carried out against Paul at Lystra when some Jews from Antioch and Iconium incited a mob which stoned Paul, dragged him out of the city and left him for dead. Paul, however, recovered (14:19-20).

One access Paul has to a direct experience of the historical Jesus is through the death of Stephen. According to Luke's theological vision, the deaths of Jesus and Stephen have so deep a cor-

---

political affiliation available to a Jewish Hellenist, see Martin Hengel, "The Hellenists and Their Expulsion from Jerusalem," *Acts and the History of Earliest Christianity,* trans. John Bowden (Philadelphia: Fortress Press, 1980) 71–80; C.F.D. Moule, "Once More, Who Were the Hellenists?" *Expository Times* 70 (1958–1959) 100–02; Raymond E. Brown, S.S., "Not Jewish Christianity and Gentile Christianity but Types of Jewish/Gentile Christianity," *Catholic Biblical Quarterly* 45 (January 1983) 74–79.

respondence that to have heard and seen the death of Stephen is to have witnessed the death of Jesus. The detail that the young man Saul was present at Stephen's death is less an accusation against Paul for being an accessory to the murder of an innocent man. Rather, his presence is a theological assertion about the integrity of Paul's identity as a witness to Jesus.

Saul is a bystander at Stephen's execution, a witness watching him being stoned and hearing his prayer (7:59-60). Later in Acts this point of view radically shifts, and a repentant Paul remembers this incident. Paul suggests to Jesus in the Temple vision that his involvement in Stephen's death is the reason his own preaching is rejected in Jerusalem (22:20). It is to this moment of Stephen's execution and prayer that Paul refers when he says to Jesus "your witness Stephen" (22:20). Apparently, members of the Church loyal to Stephen remember Paul's part in his death, and never let Paul forget.

While Luke's perspective redeems Paul's culpability, it is also true that the first appearance of Saul in association with Stephen's death launches his career as a man accused of many violations of justice and law. One reading of Paul's early life polarizes his character. Before, he is a persecutor, and later, he is a champion of the Church's cause.[3]

II. Paul's Damascus Experience and Return to Jerusalem (Acts 9:1-30)

Paul's portrait as a man accused, however, recaptures the complexity of his relationships with both religious leadership in Jerusalem and the Jewish-Christian community residing there. From the Jewish-Christian perspective, how could Paul, even after his

---

[3]See Beverly R. Gaventa, *From Darkness to Light: Aspects of Conversion in the New Testament* (Philadelphia: Fortress Press, 1986) 92. She maintains that "the conversion of Paul may be definitive of Luke's view of Paul but not of Luke's view of conversion. Nothing in Luke's narrative suggests that other converts are to follow Paul's pattern or that Paul follows some Lukan pattern of conversion." *Paul the Accused* argues the opposite position, that Paul's life is offered by Luke to the Church as a paradigm for the meaning of conversion, mission, and witness.

Damascus experience, ever have hoped for acceptance, given his crimes against the community with which he now claims affiliation? Even the narrator of the story captures the ambiguities that haunted Paul's later claim to be an agent of Jesus. Luke's narrative incorporates the accusation against Paul: "And Saul was consenting to his [Stephen's] death" (8:1).

In contrast to the loving grief of Stephen's companions, Saul continues his destructive course of religious reform as though that death unleashed even greater violence within him. Saul "was ravaging the Church" (8:3). Saul's fanaticism personifies the persecution that arose against the Church in Jerusalem. It is Saul in particular who enters house after house, dragging off men and women and putting them in prison (8:3). Saul had suffered no physical harm from them, and never had been the target of their assault. Still, he hunts them down, breaks up families, robs them of any sense of security, and doubtless throws many people into economic ruin. It is not against the Roman occupiers of Jerusalem that he directs his attacks, but against his own people.

Luke's single text (8:3) compresses into one verse a terrifying period of social and religious chaos which polarized members of the Jewish community against each other. Many households suffered from Paul's activities as their members were accused, tried, imprisoned, and threatened with death. A community already disempowered by Roman occupation is made more vulnerable because of Saul's campaign.

The fanatical, destructive energy of Saul was not spent by his reign of terror in Jerusalem. "Still breathing threats and murder" (9:1), Saul himself initiates a project of larger dimensions against the followers of the Way in Damascus. He has no particular individuals he wants to track down, only an accusation to levy and a punishment to inflict for religious deviation, should any deviants be found. His project has an anonymous and diffuse character. According to Luke, Saul was not even sure if there were any followers of the Way in Damascus, or if they were men or women. He obtained blanket permission that "if he found any belonging to the Way, men or women, he might bring them bound to Jerusalem" (9:2).

That Saul had already gained notoriety and aroused the hostility of many people in Jerusalem is confirmed by Ananias: "Lord,

I have heard from many about this man, how much evil he has done to thy saints at Jerusalem" (9:13). Saul's actions, authorized by the chief priests in Jerusalem, are regarded as a violation by the members of the Church. What was legal in Saul's eyes has caused suffering to an entire community.

After Saul's reception by Ananias into the communty of those believing in Jesus (9:17-19), he preaches in the synagogues at Damascus. "Is this not the man who made havoc in Jerusalem of those who called on this name?" (9:21) All his hearers in Damascus remember his past conduct and know his original purpose in coming to Damascus. It seems that Saul's change of heart toward the Church has been more easily accomplished than the converse. Understandably, he is met with resistance by a Jewish community whose majority is solidly united against him. Taking a stance to protect all its members from the investigator, the Jewish community sides with the faction which believes in Jesus. "And he has come here for this purpose to bring them bound before the chief priests" (9:21). If there are believers in Jesus within the synagogue, they are not identified by the majority. The Jews of Damascus, it seems, close ranks. They refuse Saul's preaching that Jesus is the Christ and they plot to kill him (9:23). His disciples, presumably a minority, rescue him and lower him over the wall in a basket (9:24).

Very early in Paul's career, immediately after his baptism, he finds his role reversed. If he used to hunt down others, he has now become one of the hunted. What he visited upon the Christian community becomes his lot as well. What constituted his former mission later forms the basis for accusations against him. What he did to bring about religious reform is perceived as treachery and destruction against his own people.

III. Paul's Hellenist Opponents in Jerusalem

When Saul arrives back in Jerusalem (9:26), it is therefore understandable that the disciples would feel strong fear, mistrust, and hostility toward him. In spite of the mediation done by Barnabas to rehabilitate Paul in the eyes of the community, he is not universally well received (9:27). The Hellenists plot to kill him

(9:29). Is it only because of theological differences with the Hellenists that Paul's life soon becomes endangered in Jerusalem? If the reputation of Saul as an evildoer was well-known in Damascus, how much stronger the accusatory climate in Jerusalem! Surely there were many families in the Jerusalem Church whose own members had suffered considerably at the hands of this very preacher. Was all that violence so easily forgiven and forgotten?

Just as he could not remain long in Damascus, Paul could not stay in Jerusalem. Why were the Hellenists so intent on killing him? Since many in the city already believed in Jesus, the content of Paul's preaching cannot have been new. It may have been Paul's style of preaching so boldly (9:29) that antagonized the Hellenist Christians. Did these Hellenists belong to the same group of ethnic "outsiders" who complained earlier that their widows were overlooked and less favored than Hebrew widows (6:1)? The Hellenists may also have included the Greek-speaking deacons (6:5) who regarded Paul as an outsider on two counts: he had come to Jerusalem from Damascus, and had never been one of their community in Jerusalem. He was known in Jerusalem only as a persecutor of the Church and an enemy of the entire congregation.

Had Paul's supporters, including Barnabas, formed the majority of the Church in Jerusalem, then it is likely Saul's return there would have been a safer homecoming. In many ways, Saul was returning to a city he knew well. However, his religious and social alliances had been compromised by his experience on the road to Damascus. Those who used to be his friends in the Temple circle now regarded him a turncoat and betrayer. All the disciples in the Jerusalem Church mistrusted him and did not believe he was really one of them. A climate of accusation and suspicion surrounded him. His ally Barnabas may have succeeded in persuading the apostles (9:27) to authorize him to preach. But Paul's success in preaching was short-lived. Apparently he could not muster enough support from the wider Church in Jerusalem to back his preaching to the Hellenists. When his life was threatened, some members of the Church, "the brethren," ushered him out of Jerusalem, accompanied him to the port of Caesarea and put him on a boat to Tarsus, his home town in Asia (9:30).

Saul's first preaching experiences after his conversion are failures. In spite of the clarity of his inner change of heart and the reorientation of his theological mission, he is not well received. He cannot muster wide-spread support within the Church either at Damascus or in Jerusalem. In both cities, he is an outsider who cannot achieve acceptance by the community at large. He quickly succeeds in antagonizing Jews in Damascus and Hellenists in Jerusalem. Luke does not dwell on these episodes of failure, but notes them. The dynamic of suspicion, accusation, and rejection is thus set in motion from the beginning of Paul's ministry.

IV. Luke's Revision of Paul's Role
in the Mission to the Gentiles

There is a long hiatus in Paul's history after he exits the scene and is sent to Tarsus (9:30). The narrative shifts its attention to the Gentile mission undertaken by Peter. It is Peter whose encounter with Cornelius (9:32–11:18) formalizes the Church's acceptance of the uncircumcised. In ordering events in the narrative, Luke gives primacy to Peter's evangelization of Cornelius as the paradigm for the work Paul will do. But Paul also has a measure of primacy in God's communication of the divine purpose, for Ananias learns that Paul is a chosen instrument to carry God's name before the Gentiles (9:15).

At the same time, Luke acknowledges the spontaneous character of the admission of Gentiles. Quite free of any legislation on the matter, and prior to the Council of Jerusalem, the Holy Spirit fell upon the Gentiles in the middle of Peter's preaching (12:44). After the persecution following Stephen's death, Greek-speaking Christians from Cyprus and Cyrene spoke to Greeks in Antioch of Syria, the coastal port city that became a center of the Church's outreach to the Gentiles (11:20). The Gentiles were so responsive that Barnabas went from Jerusalem to investigate (11:22). Instead of casting Paul as the originator of the Gentile mission, Luke describes it as a phenomenon that erupted in several settings.

When Barnabas sees the success of the Gentile mission in Antioch of Syria, he then goes north to Tarsus to bring Saul back to the Church there. Just as Ananias had been a mediator in

Damascus, Barnabas is mediator in both Jerusalem and Antioch. Saul remains in Antioch a year (11:22-26). Thus, Luke contextualizes Paul's mission to the Gentiles within a larger ecclesial movement. Paul's mission is mandate from God, but also invitation from senior members of the Church.

Luke's account acts as defense against accusations that Paul was an outsider who started the Gentile mission on his own, in opposition to Peter. Paul's own statement in Galatians 2:7-9 describes a somewhat exclusive division of labor in which Peter was to preach to the circumcised and Paul to the uncircumcised. Paul's account tends to polarize his relationship with Peter and the Jerusalem Church. What seems evident in Acts is Luke's revision and expansion of the history of the Gentile mission so that harmony replaces polarization. The competitiveness of Paul is modified by Luke so that Paul's mission is continuous with Peter's.[4]

Saul's inaugural vision precedes Peter's vision at Joppa and his encounter with Cornelius. In this way, Paul is first in vision, but Peter is first in blessing the Gentile mission as official ecclesial policy.[5] Thus, what Paul does later in Acts seems to be an outgrowth of the direction the entire Church was taking. In Luke's carefully constructed narrative, Paul is not an originator but a follower of already established policy. He responds to the call by a delegate from Jerusalem to be a worker in the mission field. Luke portrays Paul as a companion and cooperator. No longer is he the Church's opponent or challenger. This realigned presentation of Paul precedes his formal emergence on the missionary scene in central Asia Minor in the city of Pisidian Antioch.

[4]See the succinct summary of the historical reliability of both Paul's account of himself in Galatians and Luke's in Acts, Raymond E. Brown and John P. Meier, *Antioch and Rome: New Testament Cradles of Catholic Christianity* (New York: Paulist Press, 1983) 28-29.

[5]On the Cornelius episode see J. Duncan M. Derrett, "Clean and Unclean Animals (Acts 10:15, 11:9): Peter's Pronouncing Power Observed," *Studies in the New Testament* (Leiden, N.Y.: E. J. Brill, 1989) 5:171-87. First published in *Heythrop Journal* 29 (1988) 205-21.

V. Paul's Sermon in Antioch
and Luke's Pattern of Narration

Besides demonstrating the rehabilitation of Paul, the episode of his preaching at Antioch in Pisidia (13:14-52) inaugurates the realization of another aim of Luke. The evangelist begins to employ a type-scene or pattern of narration that repeats itself all along the missionary circuit.[6] The repetitive structure of Paul's experiences of preaching always involves opposition from some group or another. Luke orders the sequence of events so that Paul has (1) a beginning in a synagogue with a Jewish audience, a sphere of activity which shifts to (2) an engagement of mixed audience which includes non-Jews or Gentiles, (3) a dispute over either religious or political matters which involves accusations against Paul being carried into the civil forum, (4) an informal or formal arrest, juridical process and/or punishment which results in (5) Paul's leaving town and moving on to evangelize new territory. The cities and anecdotal details may change, but the pattern is consistent. Paul is always accused and opposed by some group, and this catapults his message into a wider audience than his original hearers within the synagogue.[7] He ends up facing secular officials and defending himself against both religious and civil accusations. Gradually, the accusations become more politicized as he moves beyond the reach of the religious authorities.

Paul addresses Jews in the synagogue at Antioch in Pisidia (in Asia Minor) on the first missionary journey to which he was commissioned by the Church in Antioch, Syria, along with Barnabas and companions.[8] It is on this journey, after the encounter on

---

[6]Robert C. Tannehill, *The Narrative Unity of Luke-Acts: A Literary Interpretation,* Vol. 2, *The Acts of the Apostles* (Minneapolis: Fortress Press, 1990) 226, calls type-scenes certain patterns that recur in Acts, e.g., a) Paul's rejection of disbelieving Jews and turning to Gentiles (222); b) the epiphanic commissioning story, e.g., 18:9-10 (223-24); and c) a scene of public accusation before an official, e.g., before Gallio, similar to 16:19-24 and 17:5-9.

[7]See the discussion of opposition to Paul and Luke's irenic rather than polemical perspective in Robert L. Brawley, *Luke-Acts and the Jews: Conflict, Apology, and Conciliation* (Atlanta: Scholars Press, 1987).

[8]Sherman E. Johnson, "Antioch," *Paul the Apostle and His Cities* (Wilmington: Glazier, 1987) 44-56.

Cyprus with Sergius Paulus (13:4-12), that Saul becomes known in the narrative as Paul. This is the first formal address that Paul makes as a major figure in Acts. Earlier, his dialogue had been reproduced (9:4-5); his preaching summarized (9:20, 22, 29), and the dangers to his life reported (9:23, 29). But at Antioch in Pisidia, he has found his own voice within the story of the Church: "Then God removed him and raised up David as their king; on his behalf God said, giving witness, 'I have found David, son of Jesse, to be a man according to my heart who will fulfill my every wish' " (13:22). One thing significant about this reference to David is the correspondence to Davidic references in other places in Acts. They occur in Peter's address to the community prior to Matthias' selection (1:16), Peter's Pentecost speech (2:25-34), the prayer of the community following Peter and John's release (4:25), and Stephen's speech (7:45-46). After the references in Paul's discourse (13:22, 34, 36) James once more refers to David (15:16). After this point in Acts, there are no more references to David.

Of note is the assignment of the Davidic references, not to the narrator, to accusers, or to Gentile speakers, but mainly to those in Acts who are the principal spokespersons for the gospel: Peter, the community, Stephen, Paul, and James. The fact that Paul uses three references to David makes clear to his hearers that his doctrine is representative of the main line of the Church's official teaching, rooted in its Jewish tradition. God is a witness to that tradition, even as Paul is its communicator.

Paul proclaimed, "But God raised him from the dead; and for many days he appeared to those who came up with him from Galilee to Jerusalem, who are now his witnesses to the people" (13:30-31). Paul seems to refer to "those" who are witnesses as those of Peter's company, those Peter has identified as "we" (1:21; 2:32; 3:15; 5:32; 10:39, 42). Tension lies between these statements of Peter and the original commission of Jesus: "You shall be my witnesses" addressed to more than the Twelve (1:8). If the question is, Who are the first-named witnesses to the resurrection who are conscious of their role? then "witnesses" refers to Peter and the Jerusalem company. If the question is, Who are the official witnesses to Jesus and his message? then this includes Paul.

Paul exercises a double role in the address at Antioch. He cites the testimony of official witnesses, and he is included among them because of his own official, commissioned role as a missionary delegate from Antioch (13:2-4). When he refers to the witnesses who are connected with the historical events of Jesus' death and resurrection, he acknowledges the testimony of other witnesses. Paul gives voice to the mainstream, officially endorsed message of the leadership in Jerusalem. Luke is at pains in Acts to contextualize Paul's activity within a movement happening in the Jerusalem Church and enunciated by its chief spokespersons.[9]

Luke's understanding of official witness must be seen in his identification of witness and discipleship. Luke considers witness to be provided on a number of bases: (1) the historical and temporal base which can be testified to by Peter and the first companions of Jesus, (2) the official role as witness-messenger, or repeater of the testimony appointed by Church communities (Matthias was chosen by the Jerusalem community. Paul and Barnabas were delegated by the Antioch community), and (3) the prophetic commissioning as witness communicated directly by Jesus to the apostles at a specific time before the Ascension, or at a specific time after the Ascension as Jesus commissioned Paul.

The functions of a witness in a juridical sense are several and Luke draws upon them all. Witnesses speak for or against a person who is on trial and corroborate testimony being given by other witnesses. They offer a countering testimony to those who bring accusations and provide evidence that will convince a judge. In all cases, they speak from the experience of what they have seen and heard.

In an extended sense of witness, Luke considers a variety of experiences as subject matter for "what has been seen and heard."

---

[9]See F. F. Bruce, "The Speeches in Acts—Thirty Years After," *Reconciliation and Hope: New Testament Essays on Atonement and Eschatology,* ed. Robert Banks. Presented to L. L. Morris on his Sixtieth Birthday (Exeter: Paternoster Press, 1974) 63. Bruce says Paul's Pisidian speech was reflective of Paul, not made up by Luke. The speech can be paralleled with the Pauline letters, and other than this speech, Luke betrays no knowledge of the letters; it is set in the context of a "we" section, suggesting the possibility of the narrator being a witness. See also Joachim Pillai, *Apostolic Interpretation of History* (Hicksville, N.Y.: Exposition Press, 1980).

These can include disciples' personal experiences of having seen and spoken to the living Jesus, which those eligible for replacing Judas could supply (1:21-22). The memory can include historical data about Jesus provided by the apostles, as in Peter's sermon at Pentecost (2:22-36). Witnesses can insist on a defense of Jesus' cause and maintain his innocence in a public confrontation (2:14-16; 13:28). Witnessess face religious as well as civil authorities on the issue of whether Jesus is alive (4:8-12). Witnesses persevere in their stance and their testimony despite legal action taken against them (4:19-20; 5:27-32). They repeat the historical facts about Jesus which they have learned from others. At Antioch in Pisidia, Paul reviews historical data about Jesus and hands on the catechesis about Jesus that he has acquired.

In the sermon at Antioch in Pisidia, Paul's charismatic individualism is muted. On mission with Barnabas and other companions, he voices the official message which Peter himself might have delivered to the same audience. Luke portrays Paul as a faithful transmitter of the Petrine doctrine about Jesus. This is one of Luke's strategies for minimizing Paul's individualism and emphasizing his ecclesial and doctrinal orthodoxy.[10]

In portraying Paul at Antioch, Luke also begins to construct a pattern which will emerge as a type-scene controlling the narrative of Paul's missionary journeys. Paul preaches first in the synagogue to Jews (13:15). The audience includes non-Jews who are sympathizers and converts (13:43). The religious message begins to affect the civilian population, for almost the whole city gathers (13:44). Opposition to Paul rises at this point until a persecution against Paul and Barnabas is launched from the civilian quarter, which includes high-standing women and leading men (13:50). The major issue seems to have been resentment at the disciples' popularity (13:45) and Paul's vehement devotion to a mission to

---

[10]See F. F. Bruce, *The Acts of the Apostles: The Greek Text with Introduction and Commentary,* 3rd rev. ed. (Grand Rapids, Mich.: William B. Eerdmans, 1990), on the relation of Peter and Paul. Some of Luke's readership may have tended to dismiss Peter, while some subordinated Paul in light of the other's significance. "Luke establishes the validity of Paul's commission by showing how his authority was confirmed by the same signs as Peter's but in doing so he vindicates Peter's commission and authority alongside Paul," 26.

the Gentiles (13:46-47). The missionaries are driven out of Antioch and move on to the next location, Iconium (13:51). A similar pattern can be seen at work in Iconium and Lystra.

VI. *The Episode at Iconium (Acts 14:1-6)*

Prior to the Council of Jerusalem, the confrontations during Paul's first missionary journey with Barnabas at Antioch of Pisidia, Iconium, and Lystra (14:8-20) may be considered prototypical. They are models for the five-stage narrative pattern which repeats itself over and over in Paul's experience after the Council of Jerusalem. So, for example, this pattern is evident in the scene at Iconium:

    a) Conversation with Jews

        14:1 They entered together into the Jewish synagogue.

    b) Conversation which includes non-Jews

        14:1 [They] so spoke that a great company believed, both of Jews and of Greeks.

    c) Involvement in the public, civil forum

        14:4 But the people of the city were divided; some sided with the Jews, and some with the apostles.

    d) Formal or informal legal confrontation and process

        14:5 When an attempt was made by both Gentiles and Jews, with their rulers, to molest them and stone them.

    e) Transition to the next location

        14:6 They learned of it and fled to Lystra and Derbe, cities of Lycaonia, and to the surrounding country.

Accusations against Paul represent various sources of provocation. At Iconium, Paul and Barnabas "remained for a long time, speaking boldly for the Lord, who bore witness to the word of his grace, granting signs and wonders to be done by their hands" (14:3).[11] They remained because the Jewish opposition turned the Gentiles against the apostles (14:2). Paul and Barnabas were at pains to correct the misunderstanding, but in spite of positive effects of their work, the people in the city remained divided against them.

The tension of the scene is underlined by the use of witness vocabulary, which reinforces the confrontational nature of the preaching. Witness vocabulary can include divine witness. God gave witness on behalf of David (13:22). At Iconium, God testifies on behalf of Paul and Barnabas (14:3). God offers witness through creation which benefits human beings (14:17). God witnesses specifically to Gentiles, showing Peter and his hearers that the gift of the Spirit is available to both Jews and Gentiles (15:8).

What God does, in Luke's view, is to establish an equivalence of legitimacy and authorization between Peter and the apostles in Jerusalem, and Paul and Barnabas in the missionary field. God's witness legitimates that of Paul and Barnabas, not as a private dispensation, but as a publicly verifiable act. There are many witnesses to the "signs and wonders" which are themselves acts of divine testimony on behalf of the missionaries. The witnessing of Paul and Barnabas is done in Iconium, however, against a hostile force which provokes division in the community. This later generates trouble in Lystra. The opposition disrupts the mission there when Paul is stoned and left for dead by his opponents who have tracked him down from Antioch and Iconium (14:19-20).[12]

VII. The Incident at Lystra (Acts 14:8-20)

Iconium may be considered the complete model for the ordering of events which form the pattern for the other confrontation

[11]Johnson, "Iconium" and "Derbe," *Paul and His Cities,* 52–65.

[12]See Arnold Ehrhardt, *The Acts of the Apostles: Ten Lectures* (Manchester: University Press, 1969) 83, on the opposition to Paul by Jewish authorities at Iconium. A great number of Jews and Greeks believed. "The apostles had to face the alternative whether the Jews should abandon their privileges, or whether the Gentile Christians should claim them." Paul is singled out by Jewish authorities, not because Luke was idealizing him, but because Paul was the chief preacher among the missionaries and "his Pharisaic training proved him superior to the local rabbis," 84.

episodes in Acts involving Paul. At Lystra (14:8-20) the sequence of events includes most, though not all, of the categories of the paradigm:

> *a) Conversation with Jews*
>
> **14:8-10** No direct mention is made of the synagogue. The lame man first addressed by Paul is cured. The man has faith but is not identified as a Jew. Presumably, he listens to Paul in an open area of the city such as the market place.
>
> *b) Conversation which includes non-Jews*
>
> **14:11** When the crowds saw what Paul had done, they lifted up their voices, saying in Lycaonian, "The gods have come down to us in the likeness of men!"
>
> *c) Involvement in the public, civil forum*
>
> **14:18-19** With these words they scarcely restrained the people from offering sacrifice to them. But Jews came there from Antioch and Iconium.
>
> *d) Formal or informal legal confrontation and process*
>
> **14:19** They stoned Paul and dragged him out of the city, supposing that he was dead.
>
> *e) Transition to the next location*
>
> **14:20** The next day he went on with Barnabas to Derbe.[13]

It is not clear whether Paul's first encounter is with Jews since he is not reported to have spoken in a synagogue at Lystra. This is the usual commencement for the confrontation type-scenes. Nevertheless, this partial pattern, derived from the complete model, is also characteristic of some of the subsequent confron-

---

[13]Ehrhardt, *The Acts of the Apostles,* 84–85. The fact that Paul and Barnabas return to places where Paul had been stoned—the region of Lystra, Iconium, and Pisidian Antioch—suggests that they were not bothered on their return because the churches/communities were now separated from the synagogues (Acts 14:21-23).

tation episodes. Paul heals a lame man and receives an outburst of public acclamation. The townsfolk proclaim him and Barnabas as heaven-sent Roman divinities. Enemies from Antioch and Iconium invade the Gentile city, drag Paul out, and stone him. No one in Lystra can protect Paul.

Paul and Barnabas declare, "Yet in bestowing his benefits, (the living God) did not leave himself without witness, doing good—from heaven giving us rain and fruit-bearing times, filling us with food and our hearts with gladness" (14:17). In Lystra, Paul and Barnabas have to defend themselves against a false identification that they are Zeus and Hermes (14:11-12). They challenge the people of Lystra and the priest of Zeus, who are proclaiming them gods because of the healing of the lame man (14:8-11).

As a protest against what they consider the equivalent of cursing God or blasphemy, they tear their garments and try to clarify the identity of the one truly responsible for the healing. They themselves are not divinities, but ordinary human beings. Earlier in Acts, Peter had to make clear both to the people and the Sanhedrin that Jesus' name and power were responsible for the healing of the lame man (4:8-11). In a parallel to that event, Paul and Barnabas face the same task of correctly identifying the one responsible for the deed.

God's identity is not hidden but manifest to everyone as a giver of benefits which meet the physical and emotional needs of all people. Barnabas and Paul speak for the beneficent God of creation. They neither make a declaration of monotheism nor give a review of Jewish scriptural tradition. The main thrust of their response is an insistence that they are human, not divine beings in disguise. They claim a limited human identity but also identify themselves as bearers of a religious message. They call hearers to acknowledge God, the creator of the natural world that is home to all people.

A tension between doctrinal exhortation and the personal identity of the speaker increases as the narrative of Acts unfolds. It could be said at Pentecost that any of the Eleven might have delivered the address to the crowd, even though Peter is made spokesperson. Any two of the apostles might have made an explanation of the healing of the lame man to the people and the Sanhedrin, even though Peter and John make the defense. No particular requirement existed that the individuality of the apostle be linked with the explanation of the gospel. The exhortations could have existed on their own apart from the particular apostle to whom they were assigned.

The same is true for the discourse of Paul at Antioch in Pisidia. All these previous moments provide Luke an opportunity to summarize the official teaching which many preachers and catechists were communicating. When assigned to Peter, John, Stephen, James, Barnabas, and Paul, the teaching is legitimated and given historical roots by Luke. The naming of specific preachers proves that the origin of the teaching was "from the beginning." Its origin could be found in the words of the first generation of followers of Jesus.

After the episode at Lystra, the interrelation between speaker and testimony assumes greater intensity in Acts. Eventually, Paul's testimony before his judges cannot be disentangled from a rehearsal of the details of his own life. As Acts progresses, the content of Paul's discourse grows less concerned with doctrine about Jesus. He must rather defend his own behavior and motivation by retelling his lifestory, not the story of Jesus' suffering and death. Proclamation gives way to defense, and defense takes the form of autobiography.

Peter's defense does not involve autobiographical testimony. In their confrontations with the Sanhedrin and the people, neither he nor John must ever rehearse his own life story as authorization for what he is saying or doing. Peter and the others focus on the words and deeds of Jesus. Witnesses like Peter and John belonged to his company, eating and drinking with him after the resurrection. Their lives, however, are never described except in relation to Jesus.

When Paul spoke at Antioch of Pisidia, this apostolic anonymity made the content of his sermon representative of all apostolic preaching. In Lystra, however, Luke's attention begins to shift away from a rehearsal of apostolic doctrine about Jesus, and toward the human identity of the missionaries who are believers in God and carriers of a message of conversion. At Lystra, Paul and Barnabas do not have an opportunity to speak about Jesus. That would alienate them from their audience's capacity to grasp the testimony about Jesus or his significance. The greatest concern at Lystra is a clarification of the apostles' own personal identity.

Conclusion

Luke begins to create a consistent portrait of Paul the accused from the first mention of the young man Saul. As witness to the death of Stephen, Saul is placed on the scene of events significant to the emergence of the Church. At the same time, cause is given for the suspicion and mistrust which Paul aroused in the Church after his conversion. His history as a religious reformer working against the Church has a negative effect on his relationships with the communities in Damascus and Jerusalem. His first attempts at preaching are failures. He arouses such hostility that his supporters have to take active measures to get him out of town. Accusations and death threats accompany the early work of Paul. His problematic history makes him an outsider in many groups. Luke retells Paul's story in such a way that his mission to the Gentiles is incorporated into a larger movement taking place in the Church. By the time he appears in the synagogue at Antioch in Pisidia, he has undergone an ecclesial transformation. He is fully incorporated into the preaching and missionary activity of apostles delegated by Jerusalem.

The preaching encounters of Paul and Barnabas during their missionary journey out of Antioch of Syria (13:1–14:28) disclose a certain pattern that Luke will repeat in the narrative of the journeys after the Council of Jerusalem. The pattern or plotline shows (1) the disciples' initial acceptance by Jewish or Gentile audiences, (2) their subsequent rejection by either Jewish or Gentile audiences, (3) this opposition being brought into the civil forum, (4) the involvement of local magistrates resulting in a decision against the preachers, with (5) the result that the disciples must leave town and move on. Thus, there is a reversal from acceptance to rejection, a transformation of the forum from religious to civil, and an opposition which generates a movement of the disciples from one location to another.

3

From Philippi to Corinth

Introduction

After the Council of Jerusalem and its resolution (15:1-29), the narrative of Acts turns from Peter and definitively shifts its attention to Paul and his missionary journeys. Luke presents a series of episodes which describe Paul's involvement in a number of public confrontations at Philippi, Thessalonika, Beroea, Athens, and Corinth.[1] After a bitter disagreement with Barnabas (15:39), Paul undertakes another journey, this time in the company of Silas.[2] The pattern of acceptance, rejection, and public confrontation occurs again during the journey of Paul and Silas, just as it had manifested itself at Antioch of Pisidia, Iconium, and Lystra.

[1] Donald R. Miesner, "The Missionary Journeys Narrative: Patterns and Implications," *Perspectives on Luke-Acts,* ed. Charles H. Talbert, Special Studies Series 5 (Danville, Va.: Association of Baptist Professors of Religion, 1978) 199–214.

[2] See Paul J. Achtemeier, *The Quest for Unity in the New Testament Church: A Study in Paul and Acts* (Philadelphia: Fortress Press, 1987) 41–42. Achtemeier says that Luke knew a tradition about the division between Barnabas and Paul and offered this as a reason for the split in the mission. Luke made the split a matter of personalities rather than the more likely case, the conflict of Paul with Christian authorities in Jerusalem, the substantive issues of interpreting the apostolic decree, and disunity between Jewish and Gentile Christians.

Luke repeats not only the plot structure, but some of the elements from the Barnabas-Paul cycle. The healing of a clairvoyant girl results in a political backlash with Paul as the focus of the trouble. The disciples get caught in the disputes of Jewish factions at odds with one another. Religious issues get transformed into civil disputes. Paul is singled out and cast into the defendant role. The disciples are pursued on their journey by oppositional Jews from other cities. Civil magistrates act with different degrees of sympathy toward the disciples in handling the charges brought against them.

To judge from their identifiable and repetitive formula, the missionary journeys in Acts 14–18 have been consciously structured as a series of related episodes. The narration is spread across this underlying frame and illustrates an escalating pattern of accusation against Paul. By repetition of the pattern, Luke demonstrates Paul's move from a religious to a secular sphere of activity.

The use of the public confrontation type-scene illustrates the shift of the Pauline preaching, not from the synagogue to the Gentiles, but from the religious to the civil sphere. From the civil arena, Paul's defense moves to a specifically juridical sphere in which religious issues have assumed a public character with political consequences. The pattern of confrontation during the missionary journeys culminates in the closing chapters of Acts. There, the last portrait of Paul highlights his role as an accused witness facing an inseparably interlocked combination of religious and civil charges.

I. Philippi (Acts 16:12-40)

Following the Council of Jerusalem, there is another program of missionary visits which Paul undertakes with Silas after his break with Barnabas (15:36-40).[3] He adds as companions on the

---

[3]There is some question whether the traditional three missionary journeys is accurate as a description of the Pauline missionary program. It may be closer to the actual narrative of Acts to speak of Paul's move, after the break-up with Barnabas, from missionary base to missionary base. He resided for long periods at some locations, e.g., Corinth (eighteen months) and Ephesus (three years), prior to his arrest in Jerusalem. He endured a long delay

journey Timothy (16:1-4), as well as the *we*-narrator (16:10-17). Some scholars regard this latter companion as Luke himself; others, as a fellow-traveler with Paul who recorded the account which Luke used. Others see *we* as simply a literary convention used by narrators of adventure stories in antiquity.[4]

The confrontation scenes which follow the Council embrace the period between Paul's departure from Antioch (15:40) and his arrival in Miletus (20:15). As in the case of the ordering of events at Lystra, there is no initial contact with a Jewish audience to commence the sequence of events at Philippi. However, more specifically than in the Lystra episode, there is a specification of the charges against the disciples at Philippi: they have disturbed the peace and taught customs that violated the law. It is not clear whether "the law" refers to civil or religious statutes. The imprisonment of Paul and Silas by the magistrates could suggest that the violation of public order or of local custom falls under some kind of civil jurisdiction.

> *a) Conversation with Jews*
>
> **16:12-13** None occur, but a meeting takes place on the sabbath at a place of prayer (proseuchē).
>
> *b) Conversation which includes non-Jews*
>
> **16:13** ". . . we went outside the gate to the riverside . . . and spoke to the women. . . ."
>
> **16:14** "One who heard us was a woman named Lydia."[5]

at Caesarea where he was held in detention for two years. His final journey to Rome took several months, and once he arrived, he was under house arrest for two years. Cf. John T. Townsend, "Missionary Journeys in Acts and European Missionary Societies," *Society of Biblical Literature Seminar Papers,* ed. Kent H. Richards (Atlanta: Scholars Press, 1985) 433-37.

[4] The *we*-narrator appears in the passages of 16:10-17 (Paul's journey from Troas to Philippi), 20:5-15 (Paul's journey from Philippi to Troas to Miletus), 21:1-18 (Paul's journey from Miletus to Jerusalem), and 27:1-28:16 (Paul's last sea journey, from Caesarea to Rome). Joseph A. Fitzmyer, S.J., *Luke the Theologian: Aspects of His Teaching* (Mahwah: Paulist Press, 1989) gives a summary of the *we* sections of Acts (16-22).

[5] See G.H.R. Horsley, *New Documents Illustrating Early Christianity: A*

c) Involvement in the public, civil forum

16:19 "But when her owners saw that their hope of gain was gone, they seized Paul and Silas and dragged them into the market place before the rulers."[6]

d) Formal or informal legal confrontation and process

16:20-23 ". . . and when they had brought them to the magistrates, they said, 'These men are Jews and they are disturbing our city. They advocate customs which it is not lawful for us Romans to accept or practice' . . . they threw them into prison. . . ."

e) Transition to the next location

16:40 They exhorted them and departed.

In Philippi, the disciples are charged, not merely with a single healing which has robbed a few persons of some revenue, but with activities which have had civic consequences. After Paul healed the slave girl who had a spirit of divination (16:16-20), he was accused not of stealing property—the girl's clairvoyance—but of a trumped-up charge of disturbing the peace.[7] Paul and Barnabas

---

Review of the Greek Inscriptions and Papyri (Australia: Macquarie University, 1983) 53–54, on Lydia and the purple trade. It is possible she was not a freedwoman, but a member of a guild separate from that of the imperial household, i.e., free and independent, with access to other kinds of purple dye than the marine variety controlled by imperial monopoly.

[6]Lilian Portefaix, *Sisters Rejoice: Paul's Letter to the Philippians and Luke-Acts as seen by First-Century Philippian Women,* Coniectanea Biblica, New Testament Series 20 (Uppsala: Almqvist & Wiksell International, 1988), suggests that Acts 16:11-40 reflects the outlook of pagan women, and Luke seems to adapt the message to resonate with themes that were familiar to women who were practitioners of the cults of deities such as Dionysius, 169–73, and Isis, who was protectress of married women, healer, ideal mother and wife, and consoler for those in mourning, 116–29.

[7]As context for the suspicion in which the clairvoyant young woman would have been held in the Mediterranean world, see "Astrologers, Diviners, and Prophets," Ramsay MacMullen, *Enemies of the Roman Order: Treason, Unrest and Alienation in the Empire* (Cambridge and London: Harvard University Press, 1975) 128–51.

are not accused of being Christians who have healed a clairvoyant, but of being Jews with customs alien to the law of Rome. The Philippians interpret the visitors' Jewish identity as the equivalent of being non-Roman. Paul's protest at a private dismissal from prison, and the magistrates' responses, disprove this accusation. Paul is both Jewish and Roman (16:37-38).

The charge against the missionaries (16:20-21) may be interpreted as a sign that there existed religious conflict between Roman custom and Jewish religion. However, the civil and legal implications of this incident are highlighted by the refusal of Paul to leave town quietly. Paul demands recognition not of his religious identity as a Jew, but of his legal rights as a Roman citizen. The day following his arrest and imprisonment, the magistrates send officials with orders to let the disciples go free (16:35). Paul protests that the magistrates should come themselves to let the missionaries go. It was the magistrates who had them publicly beaten without a trial and thrown into prison even though they were Roman citizens (16:37). Paul protests not only a violation of citizenship, but also the public humiliation followed by private dismissal. He insists that civil action against the missionaries stay in the public arena and not become privatized. Hearing that they are Roman citizens, the embarrassed magistrates come, bring them out, and ask them to leave the city (16:39-40).

This episode is important for refocusing attention on the movement from private sphere to public domain in Luke's reflection. In some sense, the religious world of the synagogue represents a private forum, Here in Philippi, the transition is clearly not from Jewish rejection to Gentile acceptance, but from imprisonment to victorious and powerful release. A resurrection motif is suggested when prison doors open at midnight and the captives are freed of their shackles (16:25-34). Paul suffers physical punishment and threats to his life, only to emerge from confinement with continued energy in spite of the humiliation and injustices inflicted on him. In Philippi, the jailer and his household are converted. Paul and Silas are released. Lydia and the believers receive another visit and exhortation before Paul and Silas move on (16:40).[8]

[8]See Sir William Ramsay, *St. Paul the Traveller and the Roman Citizen*, 17th ed. (London: Hodder and Stoughton, Ltd., 1930) 214. The fact that

The incident also demonstrates Luke's aim to reconcile religious belief with political identity. Luke is not interested in persuading Rome that Christians give loyal support to the Empire. A quite different point of view is suggested by Luke's record of Paul's angry insistence that his citizenship be acknowledged. Behind the narrative, Luke actually outlines a rationale for the persecution of Christians by Roman magistrates. Christians are equated with Jews. They have customs alien to those of Roman citizens. If someone does not share the local customs of Roman colonials, this means a person has no regard for the civil law of Rome. Without respect for Roman law, one is an *out*-law or criminal. Luke underlines the fact that Paul is a Roman citizen and insists on the recognition of his rights by Roman authorities.[9] Again, the forum where Paul's religious activity is ultimately exercised is the civic and judicial. The accusations against Paul lead him to step beyond his religious world and confront representatives of the secular government on their own ground.[10]

Lydia is identified with her work most likely meant that she was regarded as a dealer of the highest rank. She probably sold garments made in Thyatira at Philippi. "She may be taken as an ordinary example of the freedom with which women lived and worked both in Asia Minor and in Macedonia." Another, more recent view is that Lydia was not wealthy or socially prominent; her "household" could have consisted of slaves and relatives. Dyeing of cloth was a despised profession because of the smells associated with it, and it was typically women's work. See Luise Schottroff, "Lydia: A New Quality of Power," in *Let the Oppressed Go Free: Feminist Perspectives on the New Testament*. Trans. Annemarie S. Kidder. (Louisville, Ky.: Westminster/John Knox, 1991/1993) 131–137.

[9]On Paul's Roman citizenship and transfer to Rome, see Harry W. Tajra, *The Trial of St. Paul: A Juridical Exegesis of the Second Half of the Acts of the Apostles* (Tübingen: J.C.B. Mohr/Paul Siebeck, 1989) 81–89. Paul probably carried an "identity card" which would have been either a wooden or metal diptych with a copy of his birth registration.

[10]There must have been a considerable period of evangelization in Philippi, for Lydia and her household were hardly baptized on the first sabbath. A certain interval must be admitted, and this "shows Luke's looseness about time." Ramsay, *St. Paul the Traveller,* 215.

II. Thessalonica (Acts 17:1-9)

In Thessalonica, the pattern of theological issues turning into civil disputes is repeated.[11] This time the accusation against the missionaries assumes a clearly political character. The disciples are charged with insubordination for refusing to obey the laws of the legitimate head of the civil government. They are treasonous because they declare their allegiance to another leader within the empire as their king. These charges reflect a misunderstanding that could result from claiming that Jesus was alive and that he was a king, for such a proclamation might indeed be heard by outsiders as the beginning of civil insurrection.[12] The pattern of Paul's missionary tour is replicated at Thessalonica:

> *a) Conversation with Jews*
>
> **17:1-2** "There was a synagogue of the Jews. . . . And Paul went in . . . and for three sabbaths he argued with them from the scriptures."
>
> *b) Conversation which includes non-Jews*
>
> **17:4** ". . . a great many of the devout Greeks and not a few of the leading women."[13]

---

[11]See Sherman E. Johnson, "Thessalonika," *Paul the Apostle and His Cities* (Wilmington: Glazier, 1987) 76–80.

[12]On Thessalonica and the success of the mission, see 1 Thessalonians 1:9; see also Tajra, *The Trial of St. Paul,* 31–35, who notes the seriousness of the accusations. The adversaries say the preaching is a challenge to officially recognized Jewish conventions, and that is sedition against Caesar, a conscious attack on already existing imperial decrees.

[13]Ramsay, *St. Paul the Traveller,* 235–36. The true reading of 17:4, referring to the synagogue at Thessalonica, requires the understanding that Paul's converts were more than just Jews, proselyte Greeks, and a few ladies. Paul's work was also done outside the synagogue. In 1 Thessalonians, the impression is that converts directly from Hellenistic culture were the majority of the church. Three sabbaths would hardly be the limit of the time Paul spent in Thessalonica. This merely notes the first phase of Paul's mission. The second stage "is much more important, when a great multitude of the general population of the city was affected."

c) *Involvement in the public, civil forum*

17:5 "The Jews . . . gathered together a crowd, set the city in an uproar."[14]

d) *Formal or informal legal confrontation and process*

17:6-7 ". . . they dragged Jason and some of the brethren before the city authorities, crying, '. . . and they are all acting against the decrees of Caesar, saying that there is another king, Jesus.' "

e) *Transition to the next location*

17:10 "The brethren immediately sent Paul and Silas away by night to Beroea."

From the viewpoint of Hellenistic Jews inimical to the Christian movement, a claim that Jesus was a living king would generate both theological and political opposition. Rival kingship would threaten the peace of the empire. Allegiance to Jesus would be considered a civil threat. Those in the Jewish community who followed Sadducean teaching would have disagreed theologically with the Pharisaic Paul's preaching about the resurrection of Jesus. These opponents might find a political charge an effective way to counter Paul's theological position. Luke asserts that the preaching of resurrection was always problematic for Paul, recalling on several occasions in Acts that the issue of Jesus' resurrection is at the heart of the charges brought against Paul in the civil court (23:6-10; 24:21; 25:19; 26:8, 23). However, such a political charge might arise just as believably from a Gentile audience un-

[14]Cf. Wayne A. Meeks, *The First Urban Christians: The Social World of the Apostle Paul* (New Haven and London: Yale University Press, 1990) 207–08, n. 175. While it may not be certain that in every city the God-fearers comprised a formal group of persons affiliated with the synagogue, the indications seem to be that in Thessalonica the Jewish communities were divided along both theological and social lines. One of the Jewish communities to whom Paul spoke included God-fearers and leading women of the city. This community was opposed by another Jewish group which Luke suggests was motivated by jealousy (17:5). Since they gathered the loungers in the marketplace into a mob to oppose Paul, the likelihood is that Paul was speaking to a congregation of a higher social class than those who opposed him.

familiar with Paul's theological tradition, to whom the kingship or spiritual leadership of Jesus would be understood as a political messianism and a call to revolt against Rome under a new Jewish leader.

Luke has a purpose other than dramatizing the rejection of the message by Jews and its acceptance by Gentiles. The incident does not illustrate the rejection of the message by Jews.[15] Large numbers of Jews in the synagogue assembly are named believers, including sympathetic Gentiles and leading women.[16] The believers are a mix of many sorts of people. Likewise, the antagonists comprise a heterogeneous assembly. They include Jews theologically opposed to Paul, the loafers of the marketplace, and the city officials who are all presumably Gentiles. The accusers, who include Jews of an opposition faction, attack a fellow Jew, Jason, on political and civic grounds. "These men who have turned the world upside down have come here also, and Jason has received them; and they are all acting against the decrees of Caesar, saying that there is another king, Jesus" (17:6-7). This accusation of treason is brought by both Jews and Gentiles against all the followers of Paul, while his adherents also comprise a mix of Jews and Gentiles. The accusation claims they defy legitimate political leader-

---

[15]Robert C. Tannehill, *The Narrative Unity of Luke-Acts: A Literary Interpretation,* Vol. 2, *The Acts of the Apostles* (Minneapolis: Fortress Press, 1990) 222. "Paul's announcement that he is going to the Gentiles indicates a shift from a synagogue-based mission, addressed to Jews and to those Gentiles attracted to Judaism, to a mission in the city at large, where the population is predominantly Gentile. The narrator makes clear that Paul's mission to Jews and Gentile God-worshipers had some success, mentioning Titius Justus . . . and Crispus. . . ."

[16]Abraham J. Malherbe, " 'Not in a Corner': Early Christian Apologetic in Acts 26:26," *Paul and the Popular Philosophers* (Minneapolis: Fortress Press, 1989) 147-63. He proposes that in Acts, Luke makes a defense of the honorable social character of Christians, counter to the standard pagan polemic that they were riff-raff and belonged to the lower classes. Luke shows the relatively high social standing of the converts to Christianity, e.g., priests (6:7), a royal treasurer (8:26-39), a centurion (10:1-48), a proconsul (13:6-12), a ruler of the synagogue (18:8). The women are reliable and honorable, too, e.g., 9:36-41; they teach (18:26), provide meeting places for the Church (12:12), come from the professional class (16:14-15), and have high official standing (17:3, 12) 149-50.

ship and Roman hegemony by naming Jesus as a king. The main point of the accusation is the politicization of the charge.[17] Scriptural interpretation (17:2) done by Paul in a local synagogue has assumed, in the space of less than a month, political consequences. Thessalonica illustrates the movement of Paul from a religious to secular audience, and from theological interpretation to political confrontation.

III. Beroea (Acts 17:10-14)

The audience at Beroea is contrasted with that of Thessalonica.[18] Those in Beroea are more receptive to Paul's preaching because they are more noble (17:11). No specification of the civil charges against the disciples is given in Beroea, where Paul's enemies from Thessalonica have tracked him down in his new missionary location. It is likely that these Thessalonians tried to incite the Beroean crowds with objections to Paul on both theological and political grounds. The Lukan paradigm of opposition and movement to the next location operates as before:

> *a) Conversation with Jews*
>
> **17:10** "Paul and Silas . . . went into the Jewish synagogue."
>
> *b) Conversation which includes non-Jews*
>
> **17:12** "Many of them therefore believed, with not a few Greek women of high standing as well as men."[19]

[17]MacMullen, *Enemies of the Roman Order,* 2. During the lifetime of Paul and afterwards, Roman emperors did not always die a natural death. Rumors of "assisted death," assassination, forced suicide, and death in battle were usual. The charge of sedition against the emperor was "in the air" and alludes to a political atmosphere of both loyalty and fear. "For every one of them the throne was a dangerous eminence."

[18]Johnson, "Beroea," *Paul the Apostle and His Cities,* 80.

[19]Ramsay, *St. Paul the Traveller,* 232. At Beroea, just as at Thessalonica, "a wider influence than the circle of the synagogue is distinctly implied, v. 12, so that we must understand that Paul preached also to the Greek population."

c) *Involvement in the public, civil forum*

17:13 " . . . the Jews of Thessalonica . . . came there too, stirring up and inciting the crowds."

d) *Formal or informal legal confrontation and process*

None

e) *Transition to the next location*

17:14 "Then the brethren immediately sent Paul off on his way to the sea, but Silas and Timothy remained there."

Beroea is the only location along the mission circuit where Paul's hearers examine the Scriptures daily, not only on the sabbath, to see if his interpretation is true (17:11). The fact that they believed Paul after their own investigation of the Scriptures implies that they were not only eager, but literate. Since women of high standing as well as men responded to Paul, the situation must have seemed favorable. Disturbance did not arise from within the synagogue itself. Those who read the Scriptures were not the ones to become openly divided in their opinion about Paul's preaching. The source of the trouble came from outside Beroea, in the person of Paul's enemies from Thessalonica. Their antagonism toward Paul must have been vehement. They stirred up the crowds, but there is no report of any action taken by the people of Beroea against the disciples.

The source of the trouble seems to have been Paul himself, for Paul is the only one to be sent off on a boat.[20] Silas and Timothy remain in the town, which has already proven its hospitality to their preaching. The accusations against Paul are not confined to one location; the religious and civil charges against him pursue him from city to city. It is not clear whether these objections arise because of his personal history. In Thessalonica and Beroea,

---

[20]Tannehill, *The Narrative Unity of Luke-Acts,* 207. " . . . Paul must quickly leave Beroea, as he had Thessalonica. This pattern of persistent opposition that reaches beyond the local scene, following Paul on his mission, previously appeared in 14:9, where Jews from Antioch and Iconium attacked Paul in Lystra."

it seems, they are connected with his success in preaching and the content of his message about Jesus (17:6-7). Paul's supporters do not wait for enemies from within Beroea or from another city to turn the Beroeans against him. They send him away before this happens, no doubt educated by their previous experience of Paul's ability to generate conflict.

IV. Athens (Acts 17:16-34)

As a group, the Jews of Beroea responded well to Paul before his enemies arrived. The Greeks in Athens, however, do not give Paul's address a favorable reception.[21] Rather, they ridicule him (17:32). A few Athenians believe—Dionysius the Areopagite, a woman named Damaris, and others with them (17:34). But this is in contrast to Thessalonica, where some of the Jews, many God-fearing Greeks, and many of the leading women believed (17:4). The disappointing results in Athens show a decline as well in the quality of Paul's reception. In Beroea, many Jews more noble than those in Thessalonica believed, together with many noble Greek women and quite a few men (17:12). Though Paul follows the same strategy in Athens, beginning in a synagogue, he is unable to elicit any vigorous response, either positive or negative, to his preaching.

a) *Conversation with Jews*

17:17 "So he argued in the synagogue with the Jews."

b) *Conversation which includes non-Jews*

17:18 "Some also of the Epicurean and Stoic philosophers met him."

c) *Involvement in the public, civil forum*

17:19 "And they took hold of him and brought him to the Areopagus."

---

[21] Johnson, "Athens," *Paul the Apostle and His Cities,* 85-93.

d) Formal or informal legal confrontation and process

17:22 "So Paul, standing in the middle of the Areopagus, said: 'Men of Athens. . . .' "[22]

e) Transition to the next location

18:1 "After this he left Athens and went to Corinth."

Though Paul's audience in Athens is manifestly Gentile, Paul has less success in this city than in his previous efforts. His great sermon falls flat. He is not vigorously opposed, only mocked for his testimony to the resurrection from the dead (17:32). No parties of opposition form. No one takes his message so seriously that antagonism toward him erupts. No enemies from another city arrive to polarize the crowds. Paul may have wished for such clarity, but was unable to engage the interest of any but a small number. The Lukan paradigm ironically dramatizes the failure of Paul to reach his audience.[23] No synagogue factions generate a theological debate. No civilian crowds trump up accusations. No magistrates appear to take Paul into custody. Paul is not driven out of town in fear for his life; he just leaves of his own accord. The paradigm suggests a decline in Paul's effectiveness as a preacher. He gains very few converts in proportion to the number of persons he addresses in the marketplace and at the Areopagus.

[22]It is possible that the speech to the public is in fact a defense speech before the Athenian magistrates. Cf. T. D. Barnes, "Legislation Against the Christians," *Journal of Roman Studies* 58 (1968) 49: "Later, in Athens, Paul was seized (this time without any intervention by the Jews) and taken before the Areopagus. Accused of introducing a new religion, he acquitted himself by claiming that his was not a new God but one who already possessed an altar in the city." See also T. D. Barnes, "An Apostle on Trial," *Journal of Theological Studies* 20 (1969) 407–19.

[23]At Athens, Paul is not subjected to a trial before judicial magistrates. Rather, the interrogation comes in the midst of a great university, where he presents his credentials and message as a visiting lecturer before educational magistrates whose job is to regulate the lectures "in the interest of public order and morality." This is a secular authority, not specifically religious nor judicial. See Ramsay, *St. Paul the Traveller*, 246–47.

V. Corinth (Acts 18:1-17)

It is possible that philosophical discussion may have turned into a political confrontation in Athens. Luke may be recasting as a sermon (17:22-31) what was in fact a defense speech of Paul. It may have begun when Athenian philosophers took hold of him and required of him a more formal defense of his message (17:19). However, the case is much clearer in Corinth that Paul faced a formal court appearance before a judge. This was not merely a summary hearing and disciplinary action conducted by the city magistrates, as in Thessalonica (17:6-8). In Corinth, Paul has a juridical appearance before the Roman proconsul, Gallio. Accusations are formally brought against Paul personally. This clarity of the charge shows an evolution in the precision of the accusations against Paul. There had been a lack of clarity about the reasons missionaries were opposed in Iconium (14:4-5) and in Lystra (14:18-19). Some ambiguity surrounds the challenge to Paul in Athens (17:19). In Corinth, the Lukan paradigm illustrates the evolution of the accusations, with an emphasis on the juridical consequences for Paul:

a) Conversation with Jews

18:2 "And he found a Jew named Aquila . . . with his wife Priscilla. . . ."

18:4 "Ane he argued in the synagogue every sabbath."

18:8 "Crispus, the ruler of the synagogue, believed in the Lord, together with all his household."

b) Conversation which includes non-Jews

18:4 ". . . and persuaded Jews and Greeks."

18:7 "And he left there and went to the house of a man named Titius Justus, a worshiper of God. . . ."

18:8 ". . . and many of the Corinthians . . . believed. . . ."

   c) *Involvement in the public, civil forum*

   18:12   "But when Gallio was proconsul of Achaia,
   the Jews made a united attack upon Paul. . . ."[24]

   d) *Formal or informal legal confrontation and process*

   18:12-13   ". . . and brought him before the tribunal, saying, 'This man is persuading men to worship
   God contrary to the law.' "

   e) *Transition to the next location*

   18:18   "After this, Paul stayed many days longer,
   and then took leave of the brethren and sailed for
   Syria. . . ."

At Corinth, Paul meets Aquila and Priscilla (18:2), but his missionary companions Silas and Timothy do not arrive until Paul's
preaching is well underway (18:5).[25] "When Silas and Timothy
came down from Macedonia, Paul was absorbed in preaching and
witnessing to the Jews that Jesus was the Messiah" (18:5). Luke
heightens the expectation of a political clash by noting that Paul
initially finds refuge with Aquila and Priscilla, who themselves
had suffered discrimination because they were Jewish, and had
been forced to leave Rome by decree of Claudius (18:2).[26]
   Eventually, Paul's traveling companions did arrive, but whatever the subject of the opposition in the synagogue audience in
the meantime, Paul's response was violent. As Paul saw it, they

[24] On Gallio, see Jerome Murphy-O'Connor, *St. Paul's Corinth* (Wilmington: Glazier, 1983) 141–52. "This assertion that Paul's ministry in Corinth
overlapped, at least in part, with the term of office of the Roman governor
Gallio is the lynch-pin of Pauline chronology. It is the one link between the
Apostle's career and general history that is accepted by all scholars," 141.

[25] As a commentary on both Acts 18:3 and Acts 20:34—references to Paul's
work and pride in his self-sufficiency—see "Paul's Life as an Artisan-
Missionary," Ronald F. Hock, *The Social Context of Paul's Ministry: Tent-
making and Apostleship* (Philadelphia: Fortress Press, 1980).

[26] See the commentary on the anti-Semitic response of Claudius to the Jewish
petitioners from Alexandria in H. Idris Bell, *Jews and Christians in Egypt:
The Jewish Trouble in Alexandria and the Athanasian Controversy* (Oxford,
Eng.: Oxford University Press, 1924) 10–22.

blasphemed. He tore his garments, cursed them, declared his innocence, and said he would go to Gentiles instead (18:6). Not all in the synagogue rejected his message, however. The head of the synagogue believed, as well as some of the Jewish Corinthians. The next-door-neighbor to the synagogue, Crispus, was at least sympathetic.

The intensity of Paul's reaction may be related to several causes: the length of time Paul was in Corinth, the fact that he was alone until Silas and Timothy arrived, and the particular nature of the opposition to him that involved attacks on his character. Loyalties were split within the synagogue community. The violence of Paul's reaction may be attributed, then, not to a threat to his physical well-being, but to personalized attacks on his character. Perhaps there were false accusations which provoked Paul's intense counter-rejection of his accusers. Apparently he takes the offensive, defends his innocence and announces that he is directing his energies toward the Gentiles (18:6).[27] Nevertheless, he remains for a year and a half, reassured by a vision (18:9-10) and no doubt by many loyal disciples.

Not surprisingly, it is Paul who is the object of an attack orchestrated by a Jewish faction in Corinth, perhaps those opposed to a mission inclusive of the uncircumcised. It is obvious that Paul is supported by the head of the synagogue, Crispus (18:8), by the God-fearer Titius Justus (18:7), and by many Corinthians (18:8); but the hostility toward him cannot be mitigated.[28] In contrast with the ambiguity of the civil charges in Athens, there is a clear religious charge against Paul personally and individually in

---

[27]See Joseph B. Tyson, ed., *Luke-Acts and the Jewish People: Eight Critical Perspectives* (Minneapolis: Augsburg, 1988). Most of the essays resist the older hermeneutical tendency to equate the frustration of Paul with his rejection of Jewish audiences. The context of the missionary narrative, by contrast, records Paul's continued outreach to both Jews and Gentiles.

[28]Tannehill, *The Narrative Unity of Luke-Acts,* 222. Paul's supposed rejection of Jews in Acts, as in 13:44-47, needs to be recontextualized within the flow of Paul's mission. In Corinth " . . . the announcement and gesture are accompanied by a change of location. Paul has been preaching in the synagogue. When he begins to encounter strong public resistance, he transfers to the house of Titus Justus."

Corinth (18:13) as "this man who teaches people to worship God contrary to the law."

The judgment of Gallio is commonly used to support an argument about the nature of Luke's apologetic, that Luke is making an appeal to Rome on behalf of the church. The Jewish accusations are seen by Gallio—and by extension, Rome—as reflecting Jewish-Christian religious conflicts. Gallio's judgment demonstrates Luke's supposed argument to Rome that the Christians are not guilty of wrongdoing. The accusations against them by opponents have no basis in civil law. Gallio, who typifies the ideal Roman judge, is seen to render exemplary justice by dismissing the case against Paul and refusing to let the bench be used by colonials for settling their doctrinal disputes. Gallio proves himself an intelligent Roman. Christians and Romans stand on the same side, the innocence of one acknowledged by the intelligence of the other.

However, another reading of the episode reinforces the fact that Paul's conversation has moved from a Jewish to a non-Jewish audience, from a religious to a secular setting, and from a civilian setting to a specifically legal stage. One important qualification of the Gallio episode should be made. In light of the type-scene paradigm which controls the narrative, Luke's point is arguably neither the exemplary intelligence of Gallio, nor the castigation of the Jews as a group. Rather, Luke is structuring the story to fit a prearranged pattern of events which necessitates Paul's confrontation with civil authorities and his move from Corinth to another city.

Luke's narrative focus is really on Paul the accused, and that portrait is relevant to Luke's pastoral and theological preoccupations. The repetition of the confrontation structure in the episode of Paul's stay at Corinth has a purpose. It indicates again that a significant element of the Lukan project is to show the evolution of Christian evangelization from a more restricted religious sphere into a wider social-political sphere. In this wider dialogical framework, a conversation about many important theological issues takes place. Even though the subject is theology—the power by which the possessed are healed, resurrection, messiahship, and religious conversion—the issues inevitably take on civil ramifications and assume political consequences.

In Luke's pastoral vision, Christians like Paul accept the inevitability of their political engagement. Some juridical involvement attends their fidelity to their personal religious experience and their publicly-expressed convictions about Jesus. The point of the episode is not that Gallio gave a judgment favorable to the Christian cause. More pointedly, it is that Paul himself, without companions, had to face Roman justice because of the opposition his preaching generated. His preaching "reached the bench," i.e., the ears of Roman judges. This eventual confrontation, a kind of evangelical inevitability, characterized not only Paul's short-term preaching stints in smaller cities but even the very successful missionary endeavors of longer duration, like the year-and-a-half at Corinth.

The charges brought against Paul personally in Corinth (18:13) are the culmination of a pattern which was unfolding from Philippi (16:13-40) to Athens (17:16-34), an evolution that recapitulates the transition from Iconium to Lystra, in which a generalized opposition to the missionary team in Iconium becomes focused on Paul in Lystra. In Iconium, both Barnabas and Paul were targeted for stoning (14:5), but in Lystra it was Paul, not Barnabas, who was stoned and left for dead (14:9). A similar pattern evolves in these episodes at Philippi, Thessalonica, Beroea, Athens, and Corinth after the Council of Jerusalem. Hostility toward the missionaries as a team eventually focuses on Paul himself: "This man is persuading men to worship God contrary to the law" (18:13).

This pattern of focusing the accusation on Paul is reinforced by the gradual separation of Paul from his friends until he stands alone. From Corinth onward in the narrative, he alone faces the charges which were previously brought against the missionaries as a team and their followers. In contrast, Paul and Silas are coupled as defendants in Philippi (16:19-20). In Thessalonica, the pair are the objects of the house search by the mob, and when the mob cannot find the missionaries, they seize the followers, Jason and some of the brothers (17:5-7). At Beroea, both Paul and Silas preach as a team (17:10), but it is Paul who is attacked by Jews from Thessalonica. Paul is the one sent away while Silas and Timothy remain (17:14-15). Paul is alone at Athens, the only one to stand up before the Athenians in the Areopagus to defend his teaching (17:22ff). He leaves Athens with no companions (18:1). From Corinth to the end of Acts, Paul takes on the role of a defendant who is the focus for charges previously brought against members of the community. After this point in Acts, he never again appears with companions before the bench, but faces accusations and answers charges alone, isolated from everyone else.

Conclusion

The missionary stops in Philippi (16:12-40), Thessalonica (17:1-9), Beroea (17:10-14), Athens (17:16-34), and Corinth (18:1-17) involve Paul in a series of religious and civil confrontations. These escalate to the degree to which the civil sphere becomes engaged in the religious conflict between Paul and his opposition. Gradually, the answer Paul makes to his accusers moves from a dialogue with other Jews to an interchange with officials of the Roman government.

There are several narrative dynamics operative in these episodes taken together. The first is the clear ordering of events, an apparently conscious repetition of the confrontation pattern. The pattern increasingly defines the character of Paul's activity as an alternation between initial acceptance by some Jews and Gentiles and consequent rejection by some Jews and Gentiles. He alternates between the gaining of some followers and the antagonism of some factions of Jews and Gentiles who have power in the towns.

The second dynamic has to do with the propulsion of the message forward by means of the opposition Paul encounters. The opposition comes from a variety of causes, both theological and political. Most often, it arises from citizens within the towns Paul is visiting. Opposition is sometimes stirred up by enemies who track him down from a city he had previously visited. Eventually, either in the aftermath of the legal confrontation or in expectation of it, Paul is forced to move on to another location. As a rule, he is driven out of towns after short stays and against his will. One exception is Athens, where Paul leaves of his own accord; another is Corinth, where he stays for an extended period and also leaves without coercion.

A third dynamic has to do with the cumulative effect of describing the results of the opposition to Paul. Notice is drawn to the climactic stage of the type-scene: Paul's formal or informal legal confrontation. This ultimate stage of the narrative pattern finally assumes dominance in the closing chapters of Acts. His intermittent role of an accused man is associated in Acts with repeated instances of opposition. Accusations gradually focus on him, finally evolving into a fixed portrayal of Paul as the accused enduring an interminable series of trials. It is a process, in the closing chapters of Acts, from which he never succeeds in extricating himself.

Thus, individual instances of accusations and informal legal proceedings accumulate over the course of Paul's missionary tour with his companions after the Council of Jerusalem. After Corinth he must face a continuum of interrogations and trials. The legal process into which he finally plunges following his Jerusalem speech (22:1-22) requires his assumption of a permanent, rather than intermittent, role as defendant. The conversations about Paul and with Paul edge their way into a larger, politically-charged circle of discourse, progressively involving public magistrates, military officers, governors, the king, and finally the emperor.

In the first chapters of Acts, the legal encounters of Peter had been victorious and his missionary efforts successful. In the latter half of Acts, the missionary appeal of Paul loses its power to work the same effect. While he enters a wider and wider public circle, expanding his sphere beyond the synagogue, he seems to project less power as an individual. He loses effectiveness and cannot stem the tide of hostility rising against him.

4

Accused from Miletus to Rome

Introduction

While Paul is tremendously successful as a missionary hero in Acts, his activities are plagued by opposition from the beginning. The opposition arises from various groups: observant Jewish-Christians, Sadducean Jews of Jerusalem's ruling party, Hellenistic Jews in Jerusalem, traditionalist Jews in the diaspora, colonial Roman Gentiles and riff-raff in the cities, Gentiles practicing Roman religion, and influential Gentile women. Paul's opponents bring against him a variety of accusations, and these generate a series of conflict episodes which anticipate the more or less permanent state of confrontation into which Paul is thrust after his Jerusalem speech (22:1-22). While in some instances the nature of the accusation is unspecified, the charge brought by a particular group is sometimes identified in the Lukan text. Like the confrontation scenes, the accusations against Paul become a kind of theme in the second half of Acts.

If we pose the question, What are the complaints that propel Paul from one missionary location to another and finally bring him inevitably to Rome? we can trace a series of accusations. Religious and theological differences with Paul lie at their base. Gradually the accusations acquire a political character as the intensity of hostility to Paul becomes more determining of his fate. These accusations involve a transformation of religious differences into a variety of complaints brought against Paul in the civil forum, accusations which gradually assume a political as well as religious cast. Running parallel to the political character of the accusations is an escalation in the degree of political power held by the audience Paul confronts in civil proceedings. Accusations against Paul did not arise from isolated tensions or grow out of special circumstances of a particular missionary location. Rather, the evidence in Acts is that Paul, charismatic though he was, did not have a gift for diplomacy in confrontational settings or a talent for conciliation of disputes. He aggravated rather than ameliorated disagreements.[1] The strong opposition he triggered, as a matter of course, played itself out as a jangling undercurrent throughout his ministry. Finally, it gathered enough volume at Jerusalem to arrest Paul's movement and close down his career as a missionary at liberty to move where he willed.

Luke's portrayal of Paul the accused manifests itself with special clarity in several scenes from the last third of Acts.[2] These are Paul's farewell speech at Miletus, his address before the crowd in Jerusalem (22:1-22), his interrogation by Ananias before the Sanhedrin in Jerusalem (23:1-10), his defense before Felix about a week later in Caesarea (24:1-21), his hearing before Festus two years later in Caesarea (25:6-12), his last defense before Festus, Agrippa, and Berenice in Caesarea (26:1-32), and a final scene in Rome of Paul's conversation with the Jewish community (28:17-30).[3]

---

[1] F. F. Bruce, *The Acts of the Apostles: The Greek Text with Introduction and Commentary,* 3rd rev. ed. (Grand Rapids, Mich.: William B. Eerdmans, 1951, 1952, 1990) 23. He interprets the charge against Paul as principally one of subversive activity, stirring up unrest wherever he went.

[2] Robert L. Maddox, *The Purpose of Luke-Acts* (Göttingen: Vandenhoeck & Ruprecht, 1982) 66–90, notes that the proportion of text devoted to Paul's arrest and imprisonment is topically disproportionate to the text of Acts as a whole: "Since we have on other grounds every reason to judge that Luke composes with a careful eye to the dramatic movement and balance of his work, we may regard this long, final section as intended by the author to carry an emphasis and to form at least in some degree the goal and climax of his composition" (66).

[3] See the analysis of the trial passages in Harry W. Tajra, *The Trial of St. Paul: A Juridical Exegesis of the Second Half of the Acts of the Apostles* (Tübingen: J.C.B. Mohr/Paul Siebeck, 1989).

I. Defense Against Accusations at Miletus (Acts 20:17-35)

You yourselves know how I lived among you all the time from the first day that I set foot in Asia, serving the Lord with all humility and with tears and with trials which befell me through the plots of the Jews; how I did not shrink from declaring to you anything that was profitable, and teaching you in public and from house to house, testifying both to Jews and to Greeks of repentance to God of faith in our Lord Jesus Christ. And now, behold, I am going to Jerusalem, bound in the Spirit, not knowing what shall befall me there; except that the Holy Spirit testifies to me in every city that imprisonment and afflictions await me. But I do not account my life of any value nor as precious to myself, if only I may accomplish my course and the ministry which I received from the Lord Jesus, to testify to the gospel of the grace of God. And now, behold, I know that all you among whom I have gone preaching the kingdom will see my face no more. Therefore I testify to you this day that I am innocent of the blood of all of you, for I did not shrink from declaring to you the whole counsel of God (20:20-27).

Paul's farewell address at Miletus is highly charged with a defensive tone.[4] From the denials Paul issues, we can deduce some of the accusations against which he maintains his innocence. They include a cluster of charges against the integrity of his motivation. Some of Paul's opponents apparently maintained that he taught only what was calculated to please his audiences, changing the content of his message in accord with the cultural or religious predispositions of his hearers, and that he taught one version of the message publicly and another privately (20:20). Paul uses his status as a preacher, whose behavior was visible and subject to scrutiny by a number of elders, to challenge the accusations against him of timidity, expediency, favoritism, or preaching according to a double standard.[5]

[4]See William S. Kurz, S.J., "Acts 20," *Farewell Addresses in the New Testament,* Zacchaeus Studies: New Testament (Collegeville: The Liturgical Press, 1990) 33–51.

[5]Jan Lambrecht, "Paul's Farewell-Address at Miletus (Acts 20:17-38)," *Les Actes des Apôtres: Traditions, rédaction, théologie,* ed. J. Kremer (Leu-

Luke calls attention to the defense-oriented tone of the passage by repetition of the key word *witness* as Paul reviews his mission and recalls his commissioning of the elders. There are four uses of *witness* vocabulary, all within five verses (20:21-26).[6] Paul speaks three times of his witnessing as an activity he carries on alone (20:21, 24, 26) rather than in company with others. He is the one declaring his message to Jews and Greeks (20:21). It is a mission to solemnly testify that he has been assigned by Jesus (20:24). The fulfillment of this mission clears him of any bloodguilt (20:26).

In his Miletus speech, Paul refers only to himself as the one who is witnessing. He makes no reference to his companions or to a company of other witnesses (20:21, 24, 26). By way of contrast, Peter refers to witnessing connected with "we" three times in his Caesarea speech (10:39, 41, 42). As giving witness was linked with the prophetic testimony in Peter's speech in Caesarea (10:43), the witness of Paul is now aligned with the testimony of the Holy Spirit in Miletus (20:23). Both Paul and the Holy Spirit "solemnly witness" (20:21, 23, 24).

An emphasis on the prophetic nature of Paul's mission is one result of the linkage between the witnessing of Paul and that of the Holy Spirit. Though Paul is a witness who stands alone, the immediacy of the Holy Spirit's presence to Paul means that the missionary's work is identified with that of Peter and the "we" of Peter's company of disciples.[7] Luke tightens the comparisons

---

ven: University Press, 1978) 306-37. Luke presents Paul's manual labor as an example of how the Ephesian elders should help the poor and sick members of their church, e.g., 20:35. Luke uses the well-known tradition of Paul's economic independence as a paradigm, 321.

[6]There are three uses of the intensive *diamartyria* (20:21, 23, 24) and the ordinary form of *martyr* (20:26). The concentration of witness vocabulary suggests a basis for comparison between the Miletus address of Paul and the speech of Peter in Caesarea. In the speeech before Cornelius and his household, Peter likewise uses witness vocabulary four times within five verses (10:39-45); there is only one intensive use of the verb (10:42) and three nonintensive uses (10:39, 41, 43).

[7]On the discussion of Paul's apostolic credentials, as compared with those apostles of the Petrine company, see C. K. Barrett, *The Signs of an Apostle: The Cato Lecture* (Philadelphia: Fortress Press, 1972).

between Peter and Paul as those who carry out the Spirit's directive. At the same time, Peter and Paul are contrasted as preachers, indicated by the way they use witness vocabulary to describe their mission.

The significance of Paul's declaration that he is innocent of bloodguilt (20:26) is not clear. The meaning cannot be a denial of Paul's responsibility for shedding the blood of innocent people. He readily confesses his complicity in the death of Stephen (20:20) and other believers in Jesus (26:10). If bloodguilt has a metaphoric context, it may reflect Paul's sense that he has fulfilled his prophetic role to go on preaching even in the face of rejection. Perhaps the words of Ezekiel 3:18-20 lie behind Paul's meaning.[8] In light of God's command to the prophet to warn the wicked as well as the righteous, calling both to conversion, Paul might understand himself to be free of responsibility for their blood.

If Luke identifies Paul with Ezekiel, Paul has been faithful to the preaching mission in which he called others to repentance. He stands righteous before God because he has carried out his vocational responsibility. Paul regards himself as guiltless before any members of the community who would accuse or judge him. He has been faithful to his responsibilities as a teacher. He knows his intentions are straightforward and his behavior free of blame before God and the whole community. He makes such a declaration later in answer to Tertullus' charges before Felix in Caesarea: "I always take pains to have a clear conscience" (24:16).

At Miletus, Paul presumably addresses an exclusively Christian audience, not a hostile one. It is unlikely that the Ephesian elders have accused him since they have been invited to hear his address. Nor is it probable that the hearers who wept and kissed him at his farewell (20:37) have brought charges. Paul's tone toward his friends at Miletus is pastoral, protective, admonitory, and proof of a benefactor's care. One proof of his benign relations with his Ephesian followers is the length of time he spent in their company—three years longer than with any other congregation (20:31).

---

[8] In a conversation I had with Professor David Daube in 1986 on the meaning of Paul's claim to be free of blood guilt in the Miletus speech, Daube proposed Ezekiel 3:18-20 as the allusion.

Paul intuits the difficulties that lie ahead, voicing his sober expectation of continued accusations, for it is "imprisonment and afflictions" that await him (20:23). He anticipates growing tension and inevitable legal confrontation. From previous experience, he knows perduring tensions will be accompanied by mounting accusations from both religious leaders and civilians. In the last scenes of Acts, these accusations will enmesh Paul in a juridical process from which he will never be able to free himself. He states his innocence before the congregation at Miletus, one which never accused him of wrongdoing. Similar declarations will punctuate the drama of his later hearings before religious and civil magistrates. In less benign company, before his accusers, he will insist on his own innocence or others will affirm the same.[9] No matter his innocence, he will never be set free. "It is the witness before hostile authorities that is the essence of 'martyrdom,' and the role of the Spirit is not primarily to bring consolation and strength in physical suffering, but to inspire confessors to proclaim the Lordship of Christ with uninhibited freedom (*parrhesia*). This concept, in which inspiration of the Spirit finds expression in evangelistic witness, has deep roots in the Old Testament."[10]

The Holy Spirit's testimony that bonds and affliction await Paul is an anticipation of events in Jerusalem and Caesarea (20:23). Signaling a tragic rather than triumphant denouement for Paul, the Holy Spirit's testimony is corroborated by warnings of danger from the disciples and Asiarchs in Ephesus (19:30-31). Their prophetic warning is verified when hostile Jews in Greece plot against him. Paul must then travel to Syria by way of Macedonia, backtracking instead of proceeding by a normal route (20:3).

The Holy Spirit's message to Paul parallels the subsequent prophetic message uttered by Agabus, who binds himself and says,

[9]Paul in 23:1; the Pharisees in 23:9; Lysias in 23:29; Paul in 24:12-13, 16; 25:8, 10-11; Festus in 25:25; Agrippa and Festus in 26:31-32; Paul in 28:17-18.

[10]G.W.H. Lampe, "Martyrdom and Inspiration," *Suffering and Martyrdom in the New Testament,* ed. William Horbury and Brian McNeil (Cambridge: Cambridge University Press, 1981) 122-23: cf. Isaiah 42:1; 43:10; Daniel 12:2-3; Wisdom 3:1-8; 2 Chronicles 36:15-16. Testifying in the face of hostility and persecution according to Wisdom 3:1-8, for example, carries assurance of resurrection or immortality for the faithful witness.

"Thus will the Jews at Jerusalem bind the man that owns this belt, and deliver him into the hands of the Gentiles" (21:11). Paul's own words of readiness, "I am ready not only to be imprisoned, but even to die at Jerusalem for the name of the Lord Jesus" (21:13), are a prophecy of the same tragic certainty about the outcome of his journey.[11]

II. Paul's Last Visit to Jerusalem (Acts 21:15-40)

A cloud of accusation hangs over Paul's last attendance at a festival celebration in Jerusalem. He makes a public appearance as a pious Jew, going to the Temple to participate in its rituals, partly to make answer to his accusers. The Church leaders in Jerusalem rejoice in Paul's success among the Gentiles. But they remind Paul that thousands of observant Jews have become followers of Jesus, and these Jewish-Christians regard Paul as an enemy of the Law. They assume that Paul "teaches all the Jews who are among the Gentiles to forsake Moses, telling them not to circumcise their children or observe the customs" (21:21).

It is not clear what degree of support Paul has from the Church's leadership in Jerusalem. Luke interjects a reminder of the dispensation of Gentiles from circumcision endorsed at the Council of Jerusalem (21:25; cf. 15:19-20). It seems that the leaders who counsel Paul support his mission to the Gentiles, for they recall their previous decision at the Council and the letter sent to the Gentile communities. However, James and the elders claim, in effect, that thousands of Jewish Christians have no knowledge of the Church's official policy toward Gentiles. The leadership has apparently done nothing to defuse the rumors rampant in the Jewish-Christian community, that Paul disregards Jewish tradition and law.[12]

---

[11]It is difficult to find a precise metabasis, or turning point, in Acts, but it surely comes near Paul's return to Jerusalem in Acts 21:17. There are foreshadowings of the coming misfortune in Paul's speech to the elders at Miletus (20:17-35) and in the warning of Agabus (21:10-11). See Joseph B. Tyson, *The Death of Jesus in Luke-Acts* (Columbia: University of South Carolina Press, 1986) 39.

[12]Paul J. Achtemeier, *Quest for Unity in the New Testament Church: A Study in Paul and Acts* (Philadelphia: Fortress Press, 1987) 55: " . . . in-

The leaders invite Paul to make a public show of his religious fidelity by appearing in the Temple, purifying himself, and making the offering on behalf of four men who have completed the period of their Nazirite vow. The invitation is double-edged. The leaders place the burden of proof on Paul. In some respects, it is a useless answer to accusations that Paul does not live in observance of the Law. How shall one appearance in the Temple and one act of sponsorship correct a perception that thousands of Jewish Christians have of Paul? How shall all these thousands know that their suspicions about Paul are groundless? The only persons who stand to be convinced by Paul's demonstration of fidelity to Judaism are the Church's leaders themselves.

Luke minimizes the evidence of conflict between Paul and the Church's elders, but ironically suggests that Paul's religious integrity is as much their own question as that of the community at large.[13] The leaders claim to be greatly concerned about the opinion others have about Paul: "They have been told. . . . They will certainly hear . . . all will know" (21:21, 22, 24). In response to these claims, Paul cooperates with their directive and assumes responsibility as the Temple sponsor for four men completing their vows.

While his tractability certainly benefits these four, and satisfies the Jerusalem elders, it does nothing to reduce tensions with suspicious Jewish-Christians. Paul's good deed, done in obedience to Church leaders, completely backfires. His appearance in the Temple does not reduce accusations, but ignites them. Jews from Asia make a public outcry: "This is the man who is teaching men everywhere against the people and the law and this place; more-

---

stead of solving the problem of unity within the body of believers, as Luke portrayed the events, the Jerusalem conference and its decree succeeded only in splitting the Gentile mission without in any way mollifying the radical Jewish-Christians. Their opposition, as Luke himself knew (cf. Acts 21:20b-24), continued to the end of Paul's ministry."

[13]Achtemeier, *Quest for Unity,* 50–51. The question of circumcision for Gentiles was not really resolved at the Council of Jerusalem even in the irenic narrative of Acts. It comes up in Acts 21:20-21, even after delivery of the letter in 15:23-29. Thus, there is evidence that the status of Gentile converts had not yet been fully legitimated. This would have been reason enough for a split between Paul and the Jerusalem leadership.

over, he has also brought Greeks into the temple, and he has defiled this holy place'' (21:28). Paul is accused of violating everything Jewish tradition holds sacred: the identity of the chosen people, Mosaic observance and circumcision, the centrality of Jerusalem, and the ritual purity of the Temple precincts. He is almost killed (21:31) by the angry crowd.

The Roman tribune assumes he is a criminal, for he arrests him and restrains him with chains (21:33). He also assumes that Paul is a political insurrectionist. ''Are you not the Egyptian, then, who recently stirred up a revolt and led the four thousand men of the Assassins out into the wilderness?'' (21:37). Paul defends himself by declaring his real identity. He is not the Egyptian, but a Jew. He is not from Africa, but Cilicia in Asia Minor. He has not gone out into the desert with followers, but comes from Tarsus, a large city. He is not an insurrectionist or rebel, but a citizen. To the tribune he speaks the language of the Empire, Greek.

III. Paul's Defense Speech in Jerusalem (Acts 22:1-22)

By contrast, the defense speech in Hebrew before the Temple crowd in Jerusalem is an answer to the accusations Paul faced from observant Jews and Jewish-Christians.[14] The lines of defense in Paul's address are conditioned by the Jewish audience and the particular nature of its own opposition to Paul.

Paul is not an outsider to Judaism, for he grew up in Jerusalem itself. He did not invent a new teaching about the Law, nor ignore the Law, for he received his theological instruction from Gamaliel from his youth. He does not flaunt violations of religious observance, but has ever been zealous and pious. How could he once have received authorization as an investigator from Jerusalem's religious leaders if he had not been an observant Jew?

If he is guilty of any crime, it was his earlier persecution of Jewish-Christians. But that was an action sanctioned by the

---

[14]For a treatment of Paul's defense speech in Jerusalem, see Marie-Eloise Rosenblatt, ''Recurring Narration as a Lukan Literary Convention in Acts: Paul's Jerusalem Speech in Acts 22:1-22,'' *New Views on Luke and Acts,* ed. Earl Richard (Collegeville: The Liturgical Press, 1990) 94–105.

authorities. The source of his mission and teaching is not an invention of his own, but a theophany. A voice, a light, and a command from heaven directed him to see his work from a different perspective. This mission was affirmed by a devout Jew in Damascus, Ananias. It was this well-accepted Jew, speaking the language of Jewish tradition, who corroborated Paul's personal religious experience: "The God of our fathers appointed you to know his will, to see the Just One and to hear a voice from his mouth; for you will be a witness for him to all men of what you have seen and heard" (22:14-15).

Paul claimed that he had never ignored the sacredness of the Temple precincts. In fact, he had once had a deep religious experience in the Temple. During a trance, Jesus appeared to him and addressed him again (22:17-21). If Paul takes responsibility for any resistance to his preaching, it is because of the memory others have of his complicity in Stephen's death. But he makes no secret of his former life, his sorrow, or his repentance. It was a command of Jesus to go to the Gentiles.

Even though Paul counters many of the accusations of the synagogue Jews and the Jewish-Christians, his efforts are in vain. The worshipers at the Temple are then infuriated about Paul's dedication to the Gentile mission. It does not matter that Paul claims to have God's authorization to go far away to the Gentiles. The crowd begins to riot again and call for his death (22:22-23).

The Roman tribune assumes that Paul is the cause of the disturbance, but does not understand why, since Paul spoke in Hebrew to the crowd.[15] He moves to have Paul tortured by scourging so the prisoner will reveal the secret. Paul is thus treated as a criminal because the crowd has shouted against him. The tribune's ignorance about Paul becomes equivalent to an accusation of criminal behavior. To protect himself, Paul has to speak Greek again and identify himself as a Roman citizen: "Is it lawful for you to scourge a man who is a Roman citizen, and uncondemned?" (22:25). He turns quickly from his Jewish religious

---

[15] For a discussion of the language(s) spoken by Jesus and Paul, and a treatment of biliguality and triliguality in Palestine of the first century C.E., see G.H.R. Horsley, *New Documents Illustrating Early Christianity,* Vol. 5, *Linguistic Essays* (New South Wales: Macquarie University, 1989) 19-24.

identity to his secular identity as a citizen. He makes a claim, not on his theological credentials, but on his civil rights. The defense speech before the crowd had emphasized Paul's historical connections with Judaism and Jerusalem. The episode ends by catapulting Paul into a secular setting.[16]

From this point onward, Luke wishes to emphasize Paul's secular identity, rather than his religious one. Thus, there is a fourfold repetition of Paul's civilian status. He is not a Jew but a Roman (22:25, 26, 27, 29), and he did not purchase the right but was born a citizen (21:39; 22:28). His strategy in dealing with his captors is to assume his legal status as a person uncondemned by a court judgment (22:5). Before the Roman military, he thus defines his differences with fellow Jews as fundamentally a legal matter. He has not yet had a trial, and he has not yet been condemned by any formal judgment. In effect, Paul reminds the soldiers of their own duties as servants of the state, for they are to see that civil law is observed. Paul's conversation with the soldiers suggests his passage from an intra-Jewish argument to an engagement of discourse in a sphere of authority which is more powerful than religious institutions.

IV. Paul's Interrogation before the Sanhedrin in Jerusalem (Acts 23:1-10)

Having already defended himself before the Jewish public (22:1-22) and Roman military (22:24-29) in Jerusalem, Paul makes his appearance before the ultimate religious authority in Jerusalem, the Sanhedrin (23:1-10). Though the scene is clearly juridical, it is curious that in the hearing before the Sanhedrin in Jerusalem (22:30–23:10) there is no witness vocabulary. The same is true for Luke's dramatization of Paul's defense before the Sanhedrin prosecutor Tertullus and Felix in Caesarea (24:10-21). Paul's appearance before the Sanhedrin at Jerusalem (22:30–23:10) calls attention to the theological controversy over resurrection and the political-social conflict between two Jewish parties, Sadducees and Pharisees.

[16]For a discussion of Paul's Roman citizenship, see Tajra, *The Trial of St. Paul,* 81–89.

The fact of controversy is indicated by a repetition of synonyms for conflict: "dissension" (23:7); "was divided" (23:7); "uprising" (23:9); "arguing" (23:9); and "discord" (23:10). In addition, the repetition of the conflicting parties becomes a motif in the passage: Pharisees, six times (23:6—three times; 23:7, 8, 9); Sadducees, three times (23:6, 7, 8). It is the Pharisees who maintain Paul's innocence, those with whom he declares theological and social affiliation.

Paul's speech before the Sanhedrin (22:30–23:10) is a generalized claim to a clear conscience and a challenge to the legality of the proceedings (23:1-5). Paul succeeds in shifting the focus from his own alleged actions to his theological alliance with the Pharisees and his belief in resurrection. "Brethren, I am a Pharisee, a son of Pharisees; with respect to the hope and the resurrection of the dead I am on trial" (23:6). The dissension reveals that part of Paul's opposition arises from internal theological battles within Judaism.[17]

Luke's narrative suggests that Paul's Pharisaic party, composed largely of lay religious leaders, has less power at the time than its rival, the Sadducees, a social and political alliance represented by the priestly class. One of many issues on which they differ is the doctrine of life after death. This theological difference is merely a code for a cluster of conflicts affecting the position of Judaism in relation to Roman occupation. It was in the interests of the Sadducean party, for example, to make what some Jews would regard as compromises with Rome in order to retain some features of national identity. In return for keeping peace with Rome, Sadducean political control over Jewish affairs was promoted.[18]

Paul's vision of Jesus, with two instances of witness vocabulary (23:11), occurs immediately after the encounter with the Sanhedrin while he is still in Jerusalem. The words of Jesus now place Paul's mission within a clear juridical trajectory: "Take courage, for as you have testified about me at Jerusalem, so you

[17]Bruce, *The Acts of the Apostles,* 26. Luke is not anti-Jewish or anti-Pharisaic. "In his eyes, Paul the ideal Christian is also the ideal Jew."

[18]See D. B. Gowler, *Host, Guest, Enemy and Friend: Portraits of the Pharisees in Luke and Acts* (New York/Bern, Switz.: Peter Lang, 1991).

must bear witness also at Rome.'' These words are communicated to Paul between two of his interrogations, after the Sanhedrin appearance in Jerusalem and before his defense before Felix in Caesarea. The vision thus marks a geographical midpoint for Paul between appearances in a religious court in Jerusalem and a civil court at Caesarea. Jesus anticipates the work Paul will do at the destination beyond Caesarea, implying by "Rome" its secular setting. The passage of Paul from one city to another assumes a public and juridical character, and his preaching becomes the equivalent of testimony to be given in court.

After his final testimony in Jerusalem before a religious tribunal, Paul changes location. Moving beyond the boundaries controlled by religious interests, Paul defends himself in the civil court at Caesarea before Felix against charges brought by the Jerusalem religious establishment (24:1-21).

V. *Paul's Defense before Felix in Caesarea (Acts 24:1-21)*

Luke uses no witness vocabulary in dramatizing the interchange of Tertullus and Paul before Felix.[19] However, there is a marked intensification and clustering of *accusation* vocabulary in this juridical encounter: "To accuse" (24:2, 8, 13, 19); "bring formal charges" (24:1); "having examined" (24:8); "alleging" (24:9); "judge" and "being judged" (24:10, 21); "defend" (24:10); "prove" (24:13); and "confess" (24:14).

The charges brought against Paul only indirectly concern theological heresy. Instead, they take on a civil and political character. As his judges change, so do the accusations. Tertullus levels a four-part charge (24:5-6):

1) Paul is "a pestilent fellow." From a Roman perspective, this means he is the carrier of religious beliefs and practices considered alien to Roman civilization and corruptive of its social health.

2) Paul is "an agitator among all the Jews throughout the world." Besides being a threat to Rome's social health, Paul dis-

---

[19]The governorship of Felix and his style of administration is documented in the classical sources. See the overview in Tajra, *The Trial of St. Paul,* 109-16.

turbs the peace of Jews who practice their religion. The Jerusalem Jews imply that Judaism has a unity throughout the world analogous to the Roman empire. In his effort to ally the Jewish leaders with the Roman governor, Tertullus names Paul a destroyer of the peace which supposedly exists among all Jews themselves and between Judaism and Rome. Given the historical facts of intra-Jewish theological conflicts and Jewish uprisings which preceded the destruction of the Temple in A.D. 70, this claim of peace and unity is ironic.

3) Paul is "a ringleader of the sect of the Nazarenes." This is the charge which implies theological heresy, from a Jewish perspective. Paul is identified with a minority claiming Jewish identity, but rejected as heretical by Judaism. If Paul is a leader of a religious group not endorsed by Judaism, and the Nazarenes lack formal recognition by Rome as a licit religion, then Paul has made himself an alien within the Empire. Since he is not accepted by Judaism, his religion should not be accepted by Rome.

4) Paul "tried to profane the temple, but we seized him." The accusers have misunderstood Paul's intentions in coming to the Temple. Paul's effort to show that he is observant of the Law has been overlooked completely (21:24). He is again accused of the very opposite of observance, willful profanation. The charge is a condensation of the previous public outcry against Paul: "This is the man who is teaching men everywhere against the people and the law and this place; moreover he also brought Greeks into the temple, and he has defiled this holy place" (21:28).

Profaning the Temple by bringing Gentiles into the areas reserved for practicing Jews would be a violation of Roman law in Jerusalem, as well as an act of religious sacrilege. Thus, profanation of the Temple is both a religious and a civil violation.

Paul counters each of these accusations in turn. As for the charge that he agitates Jews all over the world, he says he was a worshiper in Jerusalem, not a disturber of the peace in either religious or civil settings: "It is not more than twelve days since I went up to worship at Jerusalem; and they did not find me disputing with any one or stirring up a crowd, either in the Temple or in the synagogues, or in the city" (24:11-12). Paul's contention is that he did not provoke the riot of the crowd (21:27-31) by anything he said. He focuses on the original moment of the arrest which was initiated by the misinterpretation of his actions by Jews from Asia. He apparently is not thinking of his address to the crowd and his claim of a mission to the Gentiles, which also provoked riotous behavior (22:22-23).

As for the accusation that he is a ringleader of the Nazarenes, Paul does not deny that he belongs to a special religious group. He is member of the Way, but he distinguishes the name the community gives itself from the heretical category of "sect" by which Jewish leaders identify it (24:14). He denies that he is a source of pestilence because what he believes is not alien to Jewish teaching, but identical with it.[20] He has not introduced novel doctrine into the Roman empire and crossed the boundaries of what is permitted as a licit religion recognized by Rome. He worships the same God as the Jews, believes the same teaching in Torah and the Prophets, and holds an acceptable theological position, the Pharisaic doctrine of resurrection. He maintains that he acts in good faith toward others and has reverence toward God. In other words, he is not a troublemaker or anarchist in relation to the community, nor is he a disbeliever who has contempt for religious practices (24:15-16).

As for the accusation that he profaned the Temple, he tries to clear up the misunderstanding perpetrated by the Jews from Asia. He could not have profaned the Temple if he had just purified himself. Paul does not defend himself by referring to his sponsorship of the men under vow (21:26), which he had taken on at the behest of the Church's leadership in Jerusalem. He rather calls attention to the absence of his accusers from court (24:19), the ones who charged him with profanation and who would be witnesses of his actions. The only evidence his accusers can bring to Felix in the present hearing is Paul's testimony before the Sanhedrin (22:30-23:10) when his theological position on resurrection was the issue. Ananias and the elders could attest to Paul's theological position, but there is no one who can offer an eyewitness report about his behavior in the Temple precincts.

Paul's defense before Felix is the most systematic of any of his

---

[20]Paul chooses to emphasize in Jewish theology the inclusiveness of the call to be obedient to the God of Israel.

responses to accusations. It is the first time in Acts that Paul responds directly to a specific indictment, because this is the first time that an actual catalogue of offenses has been submitted to a judge.[21] In the trial before Gallio (18:12-17), Paul had been accused of teaching people to worship God contrary to the Law. This charge could have either a religious or civil application. Gallio decided it was a religious matter, not a civil one. Paul never had to formulate a defense of himself. However, by the time he arrives in Caesarea before Felix, the former charge of his teaching against the Law has been re-honed by Paul's enemies. Now the charge implies that Paul's activities represent an attack on Roman interests. With this change of focus, the Roman governor is sure to become involved.

The trial before Felix represents the culmination of a long process of generalized opposition to Paul's teaching and public outcry against his actions, tied to specific settings. The Jewish leaders, including the high priest Ananias and the elders, have successfully transferred the opposition to Paul from Jerusalem to Caesarea. This signifies a movement of both the accusers and the judge from a religious to a civil setting. Paul's defense takes him from the theological court to the civil, secular court. Luke thus suggests that the gospel itself is moving beyond the confines of a religious world into confrontation with the state. As Paul moves into a defense before a civil judge, so does the frontier for his testimony open onto a new secular field.[22]

VI. *Paul's Hearing before Festus in Caesarea (Acts 25:6-12)*

To underline the reality of this new sphere of discourse, Luke offers a scene two years later in which Paul faces the new gover-

---

[21]Robert C. Tannehill, *The Narrative Unity of Luke-Acts: A Literary Interpretation,* Vol. 2, *The Acts of the Apostles* (Minneapolis: Fortress Press, 1990) 304. On Paul's preaching in a secular setting, "The narrator may well have been concerned to show that Paul used his imprisonment to bear witness to high officials, which would help to account for a scene in which Felix allows Paul to preach."

[22]Maddox, *The Purpose of Luke-Acts,* 67: "When we read Acts as a whole, rather than selectively, it is Paul the prisoner even more than Paul the missionary whom we are meant to remember."

nor at Caesarea, Festus (25:6-12). The hearing is actually initiated, not by Paul's accusers in Jerusalem, but by Festus himself. He invites representatives from Jerusalem to come down to Caesarea to accuse Paul (25:5).

Luke offers a chronicle of the first days of Festus in the province which guarantees his indoctrination against Paul. The governor arrives in Caesarea, and after three days, goes to Jerusalem. He learns about Paul, but never speaks to him directly. He is in Jerusalem eight or ten days while Paul's enemies have ample time to meet with the new governor and give him their version of Paul's criminality. Festus first approaches the matter of Paul's guilt or innocence on neutral ground. He knows that Paul has been held at Caesarea, but is unaware of the degree of hostility that still burns in the hearts of Paul's enemies. "If there is anything wrong about the man, let them accuse him" (25:5). Luke ironically suggests the governor's naivete, for the reader who has followed Paul's story already knows how strong is the opposition to the missionary, and how determined are the leaders in Jerusalem to kill Paul. The chief priests and elders, the narrator says, misrepresented their appeal to Festus when they asked for a trial in Jerusalem, for they intended to kill Paul (25:3). Festus never becomes aware of this intention, it seems, for he turns the chief priests' request for a Jerusalem trial into an invitation to Paul (25:9). This appears as a kind of conciliatory and friendly gesture to the Jewish leaders from Jerusalem, designed to maximize his diplomatic advantage.[23]

Immediately on his return to Caesarea, Festus calls Paul before the bench to face his accusers from Jerusalem. Luke's chronology makes it clear that Paul has no advocate and no chance of a private hearing before the interrogation actually begins. Paul has been isolated in prison. Yet his old enemies from Jerusalem, after two years, still bring the old charges. Paul makes no defense speech.

[23]Richard J. Cassidy, *Society and Politics in the Acts of the Apostles* (Maryknoll, N.Y.: Orbis, 1987) separates his discussion of Jewish opponents to Paul from the treatment of opposition to Paul from Roman authorities. He does not see Paul's treatment by Roman authorities as benign or supportive. See "Paul and the Roman Authorities in Jerusalem and Caesarea," 96-116.

Instead, his simple answer illustrates the ideological shift from religious offenses to those fraught with political ramifications (25:8): "Neither against the law of the Jews, nor against the temple, nor against Caesar have I offended at all." The "law of the Jews" implies violations of religious orthodoxy and Jewish law. "Against the Temple" concerns a religious law against bringing Gentiles into the court reserved for the circumcised, a law which is also promulgated by Roman authority in Jerusalem. "Against the temple" could also refer to Paul's teaching about the centrality or noncentrality of Temple worship for those claiming to live according to the covenant. "Against Caesar" refers to the host of politicized charges against Paul which would make him a violator of Roman civil law, from sedition to practicing a religion not permitted by Rome.

When Festus addresses Paul, it is the first time any Roman governor has ever spoken to him directly. "Do you wish to go up to Jerusalem, and there be tried on these charges before me?" (25:10). Gallio never addressed Paul or acknowledged him directly. "But when Paul was about to open his mouth, Gallio had said to the Jews . . . " (18:14). Paul's case had been presented to Felix in a letter from the Roman commander (23:26-30). Felix had not addressed Paul directly, but merely motioned to him to speak (24:10). Thus, when Festus speaks to Paul, Luke suggests that Paul has achieved a new degree of presence to Roman authority. He is passing farther from the sphere in which he is subject to the religious authorities in Jerusalem. His discourse is to be addressed to a wider audience than one defined by theological concerns.

Paul's appeal represents several thematic shifts. First, he refuses to go back to Jerusalem to be tried. It is the end of his pilgrimages to the holy city. Secondly, he asks that his case be tried in a civil court. "I am standing before Caesar's tribunal, where I ought to be tried; to the Jews I have done no wrong, as you know very well" (25:10).[24] Luke signifies Paul's definitive entry

[24]Brian E. Beck, *"Imitatio Christi* and the Lucan Passion Narrative," *Suffering and Martyrdom in the New Testament,* ed. William Horbury and Brian McNeil, 28–47. The testimonies of Jesus' innocence and those of Paul's innocence, by analogy, emphasize that their sufferings were maliciously

into a world whose ultimate authority is not religious, but political: "I appeal to Caesar" (25:11). He lays claim on the judgment of a civil official as normative for all other judgments about him: "I have done no wrong, as you know very well." Third, Paul acknowledges that the charges potentially carry a death sentence. This is not merely another occasion for a defense proving his innocence of charges, but a matter of life and death: "If then I am a wrongdoer, and have committed anything for which I deserve to die, I do not seek to escape death" (25:11). As Paul extends himself toward a final judgment by Caesar, he also anticipates the possibility of his death.[25] The constant irony of Acts reasserts itself: Paul's innocence does not save him from either imprisonment or death.

Luke's gradation in *order of audience* for Paul's defense speeches reflects a movement from less politically powerful hearers to more powerful ones. The increasing degree of power is signaled by a corresponding increase in juridical language. Luke also acknowledges the complicated web of political maneuvering into which Paul fell after his arrest. The Jewish public in Jerusalem is less powerful than the Roman military commander. The Sanhedrin is more powerful legally than the Roman military commander, even though the commander has authority to convoke the Sanhedrin (22:30). The Sadducees are more powerful within the Sanhedrin than the Pharisees. In spite of the judgment of the Pharisees in Paul's favor (23:9), the Sadducees bring their case against Paul to the civil court before Felix in Caesarea. While Felix

---

caused. "This is not good apologetic for Romans or Jews, but would encourage hard-pressed Christians to see Jesus as a pattern for themselves," 41.

[25] Fergus Millar, *The Emperor in the Roman World (31 BC–AD 337)* (London: Duckworth, 1977) 511. On Paul's appeal to Caesar, the legal basis is unclear. Paul earlier, when he was about to be beaten by Roman guards in Jerusalem, made his identity as a Roman citizen the basis of his appeal (Acts 22:25-26; 23:27). "No adequate criterion exists for checking the historicity of the narrative of Acts; as it stands it will tell us nothing about any precise rules of Roman law which may have been applicable in the area, but a lot about the power of the name of Caesar in the minds both of his subjects and of his appointees." Millar notes that Paul does not actually appeal a verdict given by the governor. The request has the character of a "rejection of one court in favour of another."

has more power than the Sadducees, as well as authority over the military, he does not resolve the matter of Paul's case. He keeps him in prison for a variety of reasons proposed by Luke: guilt and fear, greed, and appeasement of the Sadduceean lobby against Paul (25:24-27).

This shift in degree of power held by Paul's audience illustrates Luke's theological agenda. The more powerful the audience, the wider the range of Paul's message. It is necessary for Paul's audience to assume a secular character because that conveys Luke's convictions about the destiny of the gospel message, meant to be proclaimed to the furthest reaches of the earth. For Luke, this command (1:8) has both geographic and political meaning. That Paul addresses the holders of the highest human authority represents one aspect of the mission given the apostles by Jesus. To engage in a conversation with those holding such authority, Paul must confront the legal system of the empire. The courtroom is the setting where persons, not policies or doctrines, meet face to face.

VII. *Paul's Last Defense in Caesarea (Acts 26:1-32)*

Following the engagement before Festus, Paul appears before a larger assembly of political officials (25:13-26:30). His testimony is ultimately heard by an audience dominated by the civil and political authorities who derive their positions from the authority of Rome. The representative of specifically Jewish interests is a political figure, King Agrippa, not Tertullus the lawyer, the high priest, or the Sanhedrin. The audience includes Berenice, the military, and the chief citizens of Caesarea (25:23). Jewish accusers are referred to in conversation (25:24) but they are absent from the scene, an indication that the context of the accusation against Paul has moved from the religious to the civil sphere.

"They have known for a long time, and if they are willing to testify, that according to the strictest party of our religion I have lived as a Pharisee. And now I stand here on trial for hope in the promise made by God to our fathers" (26:5-6). This appearance of Paul marks the high point of the legal confrontations reported in Acts, for although the appearance before Caesar is anticipated (25:11-12; 27:24), it is never actually narrated. The encounter in Caesarea can be said to bring to fulfillment the prophecy of Jesus in Luke's eschatological discourse: "But before all this they will lay their hands on you and persecute you, delivering you up to the synagogues and prisons, and you will be brought before kings and governors for my name's sake. This will be a time for you to bear testimony. Settle it therefore in your minds, not to meditate beforehand how to answer; for I will give you a mouth and wisdom, which none of your adversaries will be able to withstand or contradict" (Luke 21:12-15).

In the continuum of the narration, the insistence with which Paul identifies himself as a Pharisee (Acts 26:5) is as much a political as a religious statement. One line in this defense emphasizes his Jewish identity as a Pharisee from his youth, as opposed to being a Sadducee, a fact to which even his accusers can testify (26:4). His Jewish credentials and previous acceptance by the religious authorities were evident from his commission by the chief priests to carry out official tasks (26:10, 12).

Another aspect of his defense emphasizes Paul's religious orthodoxy. He holds an essentially Jewish belief about resurrection from the dead (26:6, 7, 23), and affirms mainstream Jewish tradition from Moses and the Prophets (26:22, 27), thus proving he has not altered tradition. He has, in fact, carried out only what he was bidden to do by a heavenly voice speaking to him in Hebrew (26:14). God speaks to him in the same language in which Scripture is written!

A third defense emphasizes his personal righteousness and morality. He always acted in good faith in accord with his conscience, even when he had assumed that it was necessary to oppose the followers of Jesus (26:9). He underwent a moral change from earlier persecution and physical violence against others, even though these were part of a mission endorsed by religious authorities (26:10). Paul describes his change of lifestyle as a commission to call others to moral repentance (26:20).

A fourth aspect of his defense counters the politicized charges that he violates Roman law. He emphasizes that there was nothing political or seditious about his message, which was essentially moral and spiritual exhortation (26:18). If he did anything in response to the heavenly command, it was to "cease and desist" doing acts of violence to a minority, such as imprisoning good people, voting for their death penalties (26:10), forcing them under duress to commit a religious crime so that they would be proven guilty, and pursuing them outside their own geographic territory (26:11). Paul's defense implies that if he committed any actions having criminal, civil, or political implications, it was earlier in his life when he had the endorsement of the religious authorities (26:10).

The defense is really Paul's autobiography. Earlier, he had been preoccupied by his theological task as a reformer, focusing his energy on disciplining a religious minority within the synagogues. Paul changed radically after his heavenly vision and turned his evangelizing efforts to a much wider audience. Instead of an endorsement of his mission against a minority, he was given an exhortation for the many. This universal message was to be addressed to fellow Jews everywhere as well as Gentiles. As Luke reports Paul's encounter with Jesus on the road to Damascus, the words of Jesus effected not only a reorientation of Paul's misdirected zeal, but his mandate as a missionary: "But rise and stand upon your feet; for I have appeared to you for this purpose, to appoint you to serve and bear witness to the things in which you have seen me and to those in which I will appear to you, delivering you from the people and from the Gentiles—to whom I send you" (26:16-17).

After his own illumination, Paul's religious politics underwent a dramatic shift, for he understood that his mission was to "open the eyes" of both Jews and Gentiles.[26] His obedience to this new, universal mission calling everyone to repentance was proven by his immediate communication of the message to those in Damascus, then to those in Jerusalem and Judea. Finally he went to the Gentiles (26:20).

Of significance is his deletion of any reference to Ananias, in contrast with the important mediation provided by Ananias in Acts 9 and 22. When Paul speaks to political authorities who hold the highest territorial power, he describes his commission as though it comes from a single, unmediated power, Jesus. Paul's apostolic commission becomes, in each of the three narratives,

[26]The universality of salvation as "illumination," a Lukan theme in Acts, is reflected in the description of Paul's mission, as in the relation of Luke 1:79; 2:32; 3:6; 4:18 to Acts 13:41, 47; 26:18, 23; 28:26-27.

more directly an encounter between Jesus and Paul, with less and less mediation. In Acts 9, Paul could not have understood his mission without the providentially arranged intervention of Ananias, who shared a vision and a commission simultaneously with Saul. The two visions and commissions had to be brought into dialogue with one another for each element to be interpreted. In Acts 22, the participation of Ananias acted as assurance that Paul's experience along the road to Damascus had not branded him as a religious maverick. In Caesarea, Paul seems to stress his missionary credentials as coming to him directly from heaven.

Against any accusation of heresy, Paul's speech emphasizes that he has been neither a maverick nor a sectarian. The high priest and the elders had been the source of his first commission, validating his identity as a member of the Jewish establishment (26:10, 12). He emphasizes his endorsement by the religious authorities and his mandate from the heavenly voice of Jesus speaking to him in Hebrew (26:14). Luke's purpose seems less to establish Paul's credentials as an orthodox Jew than to refute the accusations brought against him previously by Tertullus (24:5-6).

By eliminating violations of Roman law from the cluster of accusations, Paul focuses the conflict on intra-Jewish religious differences over the doctrine of resurrection: "For this reason the Jews seized me in the temple and tried to kill me. To this day I have had the help that comes from God, and so I stand here testifying both to small and great, saying nothing but what the prophets and Moses said would come to pass" (26:21-22). Paul's Jewish accusers are thus co-religionists who differ with Paul over theological questions of resurrection and the inclusion or noninclusion of Gentiles in the message of salvation.

Such a move on Paul's part is an effort to extricate himself from civil charges of sedition, religious proselytism for a cult not tolerated by Rome, and profanation of the Temple. A last rhetorical effort at Caesarea succeeds in convincing his judges. He has, in their view, done nothing worthy of death or imprisonment (26:30-31). The supreme irony is that in appealing to the Roman juridical bench, Paul has short-circuited the effectiveness of his defense. In Acts 26 he has claimed innocence of any political charges. His audience judges this to be true, that he is innocent of anything over which they would have jurisdiction.

Yet Paul hinders his own vindication. To protect himself from predictable condemnation on religious charges by the Sanhedrin, he appeals to Caesar (25:10-11). He had attempted to take the discussion out of the purely religious sphere in hopes of a fairer, more impartial hearing with the focus on political charges that could not be proven.[27] Nevertheless, he had enmeshed himself in a political process, and to get free of it, he had to address the political charges and deny them. However, before Agrippa and Festus, Paul does just the reverse. He tries to focus the accusations against him back onto religious issues. A Roman tribunal would recognize that such issues were not its proper sphere of jurisdiction and would dismiss the case, as had been Paul's experience with Gallio (18:12-17). Paul's self-protective maneuver to change the venue of his trial to Rome thus backfired. Were there not in fact a political issue and a political charge, why had Paul appealed to Rome at all? By doing so, Paul placed himself in the position of having to address political charges, even though he had steadfastly maintained that the accusations against him had arisen from religious conflicts. Ironically, as Agrippa remarks, "This man could have been set free if he had not appealed to Caesar" (26:32).[28]

VIII. Accusations and Paul's Preaching in Rome (Acts 28:17-30)

The last direct encounter of Paul with Jesus reported in Acts takes place after his confrontation with the Sanhedrin while he

[27]Paul Garnsey, "The Lex Julia and Appeal Under the Empire," *Journal of Roman Studies* 56 (1966) 167–89. On Paul's motivation for the appeal, see p. 57: "St. Paul requested a trial before Nero at Rome because he knew that he would leave himself no chance if he agreed to go before the procurator's tribunal at Jerusalem."

[28]Tannehill, *The Narrative Unity of Luke-Acts,* Vol. 2, 308. On Paul's innocence: "Roman officials are quite willing to recognize Paul's innocence when they can do so cheaply, that is, when it has no effect on Paul's legal status and no political consequences. They speak of Paul's innocence as Paul passes out of their jurisdiction and they are rid of the political problem that Paul poses" (see 23:29, 25:25; 26:31-32).

is held in protective custody: "And the following night the Lord stood by him and said, 'Take courage, for as you have testified about me at Jerusalem, so you must bear witness also at Rome' " (23:11). Later, he experiences a less direct vision of the angel of God during the storm at sea on his way to Rome. While he is on ship, he is given, through the angelic messenger, God's confirmation that he will appear before Caesar. He understands that those traveling aboard ship with him will be safe (27:23-24).

The geographical shift from Jerusalem to Caesarea has signaled a major change in the scene and sphere of action. Luke establishes the political, public sphere as the new theatre for Paul's defense and installs civil authorities as the permanent new audience for the denouement of Paul's mission. Whatever Paul does is now in view of the Roman authorities. By assuming his civil, political identity when he claims the rights of his Roman citizenship (22:25-29), he has become, irrevocably, a public person in both a civil and religious sense. His preaching is now a public act unresisted by the civil authorities. Paul is unhampered to any significant degree by either the refusal of some of his hearers to accept his interpretation or their regard of his views as sectarian and separatist (28:22). The identity of his new judges emphasizes the civilian character of this world's authority.

His ability to carry out his mission in Rome, even while he is under arrest, suggests that the context of his work has undergone a radical transformation and acquired an immunity from disabling accusations.[29] Paul's preaching in Rome contrasts markedly with the ordeals of his interrogations before the Jewish crowd in Jerusalem, before the Sanhedrin, and before Felix and Festus during the hearings in Caesarea. At the end of his hearing before Agrippa, with the final appearance before Caesar still ahead of him, he has not lost conviction but gained strength. The process of enduring imprisonment for two years and periodically facing his accusers has not caused his energies to be confined within the limits of prison walls. Peter and John had experienced a burst of freedom between their two Sanhedrin trials when the angel opened the public jail and sent them back out to the Temple

---

[29]See B. M. Rapske, "The Importance of Helpers to the Imprisoned Paul in the Book of Acts," *Tynedale Bulletin* 42 (1991) 3-30.

precincts to continue teaching (5:19-20). Paul likewise experiences the freedom to continue his work in public after the last hearing at Caesarea and before his civil trial in Rome: "When they had appointed a day for him, they came to him at his lodging in great numbers. And he expounded the matter to them from morning till evening, testifying to the kingdom of God and trying to convince them about Jesus both from the law of Moses and from the prophets" (28:23).

Paul's outburst of preaching activity in Rome is signaled by a series of three verbs in close sequence, a grammatical compression that calls attention to the intensity of the missionary activity. Paul *expounded* the propositions. He *testified* to the Kingdom of God. He *convinced* his hearers about Jesus (28:23). The preaching is simultaneously annunciatory and argumentative. It is well-received by some and resisted by others in the Jewish community. It is both a success and a failure, yet carried on freely even while under house arrest. Though grounded in a Gentile setting, the message is still addressed first to a Jewish audience. When Paul arrives in Rome he recovers something of his former missionary vigor, a freedom of activity and expression which had been severely curtailed while he was in Jerusalem and Caesarea. The dynamics of both acceptance and accusation continue to manifest themselves in the reaction of his audience.

The description of Paul's preaching in Rome, however, is comparatively peaceful. This period is more tranquil, in stark contrast to the life-threatening reactions to his post-conversion preaching in Jerusalem and the attempts on his life throughout his missionary journeys.[30] The irony, of course, is that his death has already been predicted and anticipated. The sojourn in Rome allows Paul a missionary leave until his inevitable end. He emerges from the solitude he suffered in Caesarea and finds himself warmly greeted by friends (28:15). The attention he receives does not isolate him as a prisoner but marks him as the recipient of special treatment. Having his own quarters with his own guard is a distinction not granted the ordinary prisoner (28:16). Nevertheless, he is under guard.

---

[30]The attempts on Paul's life are numerous in Acts: 9:23, 24, 29; 14:19; 21:31; 22:23; 23:12, 14, 15, 21, 27, 29; 25:3; 26:21; 27:42.

Instead of charging him with crimes, the Jewish community assures Paul they have not heard about the accusations against him, and Paul's defense proves to be premature (28:21). Instead of rejecting his defense, the community listens to him and he is asked to speak to them again (28:22-23). Paul is not haled before the Jewish leaders. He remains in his own dwelling and those who are interested come to him, not to accuse him but to hear him out (28:23).

In spite of the eventual lack of interest in his teaching by some of the Jewish community, Paul's preaching and teaching are carried on without hindrance for two years (28:31).[31] He is not confined to any particular time frame or format for speaking his message. Earlier he had been held to the prescribed limits of a defense speech spoken at a designated moment in the process of official hearings. In Rome, he speaks "from morning until evening" without interruption (28:23). Though he occupies a privileged place in the public eye, Paul is never again called before a Jewish tribunal as he had been in Jerusalem. His appeal to Caesar (25:10-11) catapulted his actions and words into the public domain in such a way that they could no longer be claimed as the sole province of religious authority to judge.

Typical of his missionary journeys, Paul's preaching still arouses a mixed response. His reply reflects this variegated reaction. Luke places the citation of Isaiah 6:9 on Paul's lips (28:25-27). Paul himself speaks the words of Isaiah, in contrast to the "voice" which utters other New Testament citations of the passage. By doing so, Luke makes an editorial statement: Paul is a prophetic figure who speaks with prophetic authority. Earlier in Acts, Peter says in Jerusalem that both the witnesses and the Holy Spirit testify to the same thing (5:22). In Caesarea he says that all the prophets testify to Jesus (26:22-23). The linguistic link of witness unites the work of the companions of Peter with that of the prophets (10:43). In the last scenes of Acts, Paul's preaching is also connected with prophetic exhortation.

[31]On Paul's boldness of speech, see Abraham J. Malherbe, " 'Not in a Corner': Early Christian Apologetic in Acts 26:26," *Paul and the Popular Philosophers* (Minneapolis: Fortress Press, 1989) 160. Malherbe links this word, *parrhesia,* with the classical philosophers, who speak with confidence, fearlessness, and force, not only of words but of character.

The text from Isaiah thus highlights Paul's charismatic and prophetic authority, reminding readers of the parallel with Peter's preaching authority. Because of his connection with Peter, Paul's teaching authority is legitimated on three accounts. First, like Peter and the apostolic company, Paul is a teacher in the tradition of the prophets. He will be rejected by some, but rejection authenticates his prophetic identity. Second, the source of his teaching is not his own wisdom. Like Isaiah, Paul's mission is generated by divine initiative and election; he has been chosen beforehand (10:41; 22:15). Third, the carrying out of the prophetic task involves, as with Isaiah, speaking to hearers who share the prophet's own religious tradition and culture. Paul's audience, like that of other prophets, includes both hearers who are receptive and those slow to respond. In spite of resistance, the preaching goes on until the time when the task is completed.[32]

When Isaiah asked "how long" his work was to continue, he understood that the preaching must go on until the time of the abandonment of the cities and land (Isa 6:11-13). Until the tragedy of the Exile had proven to be definitive, Isaiah's mission would continue. The ending of Acts might represent Luke's answer to the question of how long Paul's preaching would go on. Paul's prophetic ministry to his own people would not reach its terminus until that ministry had, paradoxically, borne the fruit of reaching many Gentiles. Even though the narrative of Paul's mission through Gentile territories included a record of both acceptance and rejection by Gentiles, the time of fulfilling that mission is not yet completed in Luke's eyes.[33]

[32]See Eric Franklin, *Christ the Lord: A Study in the Purpose and Theology of Luke-Acts* (London: SPCK, 1975) 114, who qualifies the supposed indictment of Israel at the end of Acts. He believes Luke's view is focused on promoting his community's belief that God's continuing action in history began and continues with Jesus Christ. The focus is not the condemnation of one group as the means of blessing the other. "What Luke does is to try to account for Israel's disbelief in a way that does not cause a denial of her history and which leaves open her contact with God's promises." Thus, Paul is still a loyal Jew whose adherence to Christianity is the logical outcome of his earlier piety (22:3; 23:5; 24:11-16) and his concern for his own nation (21:23; 23:11; 24:17; 28:17).

[33]Tannehill, *The Narrative Unity of Luke Acts,* Vol. 2, 290, asserts that

Looking to the future, Paul anticipates that the Gentiles will hear the message. Luke the narrator knows they already have. The time for fulfillment is not conditioned, however, by acceptance from a certain pre-determined number of either Jewish or Gentile hearers. Luke's editorial comment (28:28) is that the message of Isaiah concerning God's salvation has indeed been heard and accepted by the Gentiles. Witnessing in spite of resistance, Paul proclaims a prophetic message which has reached its destined intensity and accomplished its purpose.

From this perspective, the passage from Isaiah is not condemnatory of Paul's hearers, but descriptive of the consequences of being a prophet. God's benevolent love is the force which impels the prophet, but inevitable resistance and rejection from some quarters will always attend the prophet's work. The opposition serves a purpose in God's design and time. In the time of Isaiah, the prophet was exhorting his own people to repentance. That has been Paul's message as well (26:20). In Isaiah's vision, God's benevolent purpose endures whether it is immediately seen, heard, and understood, or not. God permanently intends to reveal, to speak, to enlighten, and to heal. This divine benevolence is extended both to those who immediately understand and respond, and to those who do not. In Luke's theological perspective, God's enduring purposes are not conditioned by the changing responses of Paul's hearers. The Isaiah passage emphasizes God's healing intention, not the fact of human resistance.

On the question of the ending of Acts, the historian would question why there is no report of the death of Paul, since this would be the most appropriate conclusion to Acts. Is this the true ending or has the ending been lost? Has the narrative for some reason been left unfinished by Luke? One proposal is that Paul's death was not reported so that the life of Paul would not be cast into a questionable context, since Hellenistic audiences would

---

Luke shows Paul "speaking in a way that is sensitive to his audience in the narrative. It also shows a real concern to find ways of breaking through the wall that is being built between Judaism and Christianity. . . . Paul is presented to Christians as a resourceful witness from whom other missionaries can learn. This view does imply that there is a continuing concern in Acts with a mission to Jews, even though relations have been poisoned by controversy."

judge people's moral character by the sort of death they died. Moreover, a report of Paul's death could have been seen as an indictment of the very Roman authorities to whom Luke was supposedly making his appeal.[34]

A more likely solution is that the ending of Acts is comparable with the ending of the Gospel of Mark, which also seems unfinished. Some precautions must be taken against applying to Acts twentieth-century norms for fictional literature. Expectations of a novelistic structure including beginning, middle, and end may not apply to Luke's project. The author of any narrative must have compositional freedom to end at a place deemed artistically appropriate, and the ending of Acts should be judged in light of the whole of Acts as a narrative and theological unity. One theological point made at the end of Acts is Paul's vitality. He is continuing his preaching mission unhindered. The emphasis, rather than being on his biography, is on his mission of preaching. The kingdom of God and the identity of Jesus are still being proclaimed. In spite of opposition, legal trials, and impending death for the messenger, the dynamic of the preaching mission and the boldness of the preachers cannot be held back. The gospel is unstoppable.[35]

Conclusion

The last eight chapters of Acts sum up the effect of Paul's history of accusation and opposition. As Paul's missionary career draws to a close, he takes on the character of a man accused who will never be declared innocent. He lives through the events of

[34]G. W. Trompf, "On Why Luke Declined to Recount the Death of Paul—Acts 27-28 and Beyond," *Luke-Acts: New Perspectives from the Society of Biblical Literature Seminar,* ed. Charles H. Talbert (New York: Crossroad, 1984) 225-39.

[35]For a theological and literary perspective on the ending of Acts, see William S. Kurz, "Narrative Approaches to Luke-Acts, *Biblica* 68 (1987) 195-220. Within the historical-critical discussion of the chronology governing Luke's composition of Acts, see Colin J. Hemer, "The Ending of Acts," *The Book of Acts in the Setting of Hellenistic History* (Tübingen: J.C.B. Mohr/Paul Siebeck, 1989; Winona Lake, Ind.: Eisenbrauns, 1990) 383-404.

his public life at the edge of death. When he is giving his farewell at Miletus, Paul refers to the history of his constant harassment by plots and opposition (20:19), and anticipates that history will repeat itself in future trials (20:22-23). Conscious that this could entail imprisonment or even death in Jerusalem, he nevertheless expresses stouthearted determination to proceed with his travel plans when he lodges at Caesarea in the house of Philip (21:13).

In Jerusalem, the elders warn Paul that believing Jews in the city, still zealous for the Law, regard him as someone who encourages observant diaspora Jews to give up their traditional customs (21:20-21), and they propose a means for him to make public the fact that he observes Jewish religious law and devotional practice (21:22-24). This attempt backfires, and Paul's attendance at purification rites in the Temple is misperceived by Asian Jews, likely those from cities where he had already made enemies. The crowd's violence reaches fever pitch and they call for his death (21:36) because he has turned people away from their solidarity as Jews, away from observance of the Law, and away from the Temple. He has desecrated the Temple precincts by bringing a Gentile into the court reserved for observant Jewish men (21:28). After his arrest, Paul attempts to placate the mob with an explanation and defense, but they demonstrate vociferously and call for his death again (22:22-23).

His appearance before the Sanhedrin (23:1-10) begins and ends in violence. Ananias commands that Paul be struck on the mouth (23:2), and the tribune Lysias takes him into protective custody again to keep him from being physically harmed in the aftermath of hostilities that erupt between Sadducees and Pharisees (23:10). An assassination attempt against Paul is planned by more than forty conspirators who make public to the religious authorities their formal intention to kill him. They even ask the assistance of the high priest in maneuvering Paul into a vulnerable position so they can kill him (23:12-15).

Within the week, the Jerusalem religious establishment presses formal charges against Paul at Caesarea, through Tertullus (24:1-8). Two years later, this antagonism and determination to kill Paul are still very much alive and the change of Roman administration to Festus renews the chief priests' and elders' efforts to get Paul sent back to Jerusalem for trial so that he can be ambushed and killed on the way (25:2-3). At an appearance before Festus in Caesarea, Paul's Jewish opponents renew their charges against him and ask for the death penalty. Paul says that if he is guilty of crimes deserving the death penalty, he accepts death; but if he is not a wrongdoer, and there is no substance to the charges, he cannot be handed over to his accusers for trial simply because they accuse him (25:11).

In Festus' conversation with Agrippa, he refers to "the whole Jewish people," not merely the religious leaders who petitioned him in Jerusalem and Caesarea for a death sentence (25:24). Paul's address to Agrippa refers to these accusations by Jewish opponents and implies that they are to be understood in the religious context of Jewish customs and controversies (26:2-3). Paul says that his preaching about repentance to both Jews and Gentiles is what aroused the violence of the Temple mob against him (26:20-21).

In the last two chapters of Acts, the tide of active violence against Paul seems to recede. By the time he reaches Rome, however, he still considers it crucial to clarify where he stands with Roman Jews, fearing that charges against him may have preceded him (28:17-20). The Jewish leaders assure him that no one has sent letters about him or spoken ill of him personally, but they are aware that the teachings Paul represents are spoken against everywhere and regarded as an undesirable sect (28:22).

The final portrait Luke gives of Paul shows a man accused who is still continuing his active ministry in spite of all opposition and in spite of the certainty of his death.

Conclusion

Any reading of Acts must certainly concern itself with the character of Paul, since Luke has given over so much of the narrative to his hero. How does Paul's role in Acts offer some direction or inspiration for ministers in the Christian community, the pastors, catechists, and missionary teachers whose ecclesial responsibilities are similar to Luke's? In light of this question, determination of Luke's purpose in Acts does not focus on his attitude toward Roman government or Roman officials. Paul is not a vehicle for Luke's opinion about the Roman government. Paul is neither the enactor of Luke's positive regard for civil authority nor the personification of his fear of it because of the harm it can inflict upon the Church. Rather, the pastoral perspective calls attention to Paul as a model for community members who face struggles similar to those Paul endured as a missionary faithful to his preaching vocation. Luke's audience is composed of a wide variety of hearers, not a single group. The heterogeneous community includes members of residential families, missionary teachers, believers with Jewish backgrounds, converts from Hellenistic mystery religions, those sympathetic to the Jewish religion, Greek speakers and Aramaic speakers, those comfortable with a cosmopolitan and culturally diverse atmosphere, and those who found their identity in loyalty to the land of Israel. It is Luke's particular genius to offer Paul to this diverse community as its model for conversion, dedication to the mission of Jesus Christ, and ceaseless self-donation to the service of the growing community of faith throughout the Mediterranean.

The narrative about Paul in the last six chapters of Acts certainly expresses a particular form which personal suffering may take. The narrative of Paul's ordeals compels strong identification between the missionary and anyone who has suffered because of conflict with the political structure. If converts ever felt caught between two worlds, they could find inspiration in Paul, who incarnated the tension between fidelity to religious experience and the exigencies of living in a secular society. Paul's last years dramatize the ordeal of an innocent person's arrest, imprisonment, and trial.

These episodes of Paul's public juridical confrontations, as we have seen, gradually assume dominance as the subject of the narrative. The review of the life of Paul *the witness* focuses more and more on episodes leading up to those final scenes of Paul *the accused.* His role as a witness defending himself defines his visibility within the community of faith; his courageous self-expression in public dominates the communal memory of his life. The continuum of his missionary effort throughout the Mediterranean halts abruptly during his last visit to Jerusalem. Then the pace of the narrative slows, with Paul making only a few dramatic appearances over a four-year period. The last chapters of Acts are composed of striking, well-defined moments when Paul emerges to give a brilliant defense speech before one audience or another.

Behind these brief appearances lies a dark backdrop of lonely weeks isolated in prison as a captive awaiting trial. Luke, by force of narrative omission, makes it clear that even in a major seaport as accessible as Caesarea, no friends of Paul succeed in rescuing him from captivity over a two-year period. Abandoned by his former colleagues or suffering their helplessness, Paul was left to languish. No advocate offered legal assistance. Nothing Paul had done previously evoked any determined action to free him from prison in Caesarea—not his dizzying success on the mission tour throughout Asia and Greece, not his generous donation of money to the poor in Jerusalem, and not his proof of orthodoxy and payment of the Temple stipend for several Jews ending the period of their Nazirite vow. Though he had supported himself and had taken pride in not being a financial burden to anyone, no friends raised enough money to supply the bribe that would have satisfied the Roman governor holding him in prison.

Though Paul acknowledged his problematic life prior to his conversion, he may never have succeeded, in his life-time, in over-
coming the suspicion which many believers attached to him.
Luke's heroizing of Paul some decades after his death certainly
has as a partial aim the sympathetic contextualizing of Paul's old
life within the larger and miraculously sustained outreach of his
new life. The community as a whole now bore a sort of "family
resemblance" to Paul's spiritual vision. It had realized his dream
that the Church become home for culturally diverse groups of
Jewish and Gentile Christians. Luke is honest enough as an
historian to record that the violence against Paul throughout his
adult life was partly a reaction to his forceful and problematic
personality. Paul himself felt deep guilt at times for his complicity in the death of Stephen and his own violence against other
Jews. The jealousy of local religious leaders was provoked by
Paul's rhetorical brilliance as a well-trained, charismatically appealing rabbi.

However, Luke shapes the "causes" for Paul's suffering as the
necessary accompaniment of his role as a witness. Paul suffers
violence because he stands in the line of other prophets testifying
to the demanding yet inviting word of God. The Holy Spirit does
not spare him but does sustain him. Paul is a prophetic interpreter
of his own theological tradition in its extension of the covenant
to the Gentiles. He lives, works, and dies a loyal Jew, deeply
moved by his mystical experiences, driven to a ceaseless journeying, preoccupied with his opponents as much as consoled by his
followers, and passionately attached to Jerusalem—his spiritual
home. For two years he is engulfed by solitude. He finds, paradoxically, that the power to give witness to the gospel acquires
strength in darkness and loneliness. He bears the burden of his
accusations largely in silence. Only rarely does he enjoy that
restorative elixir which is righteous self-defense and self-
explanation. At the end of his captivity, the accusations matter
less than what they have given birth to: the definition of his spiritual history, sharpened by weeks and months of contemplation.
His gospel includes his own autobiography. His personal history
is the text of God's revelation for the community. His own story
is the heritage he hands over to his spiritual descendants.

When he sets out for Rome aboard ship, Paul has recovered

his power of geographical movement. He survives dangers at sea as he has survived them on land. Luke takes delight in rehearsing the physical indestructibility of Paul, his remarkable emotional resiliency, his compassion for the fearful, and his pastoral concern for shipmates—an optimism stronger than any storm at sea. The journey across dangerous waters is simply another metaphor of his life as a missionary. His autonomy is circumscribed in Rome and he is destined for death at an uncertain time.

Yet he continues alive to the very end of the narrative, and we are never sure how the story of his missionary career really concludes. We suspect that *death* is not the end of the story. *Life* is, after all, the destiny of those who believe in resurrection. To the very end, Paul *the accused* is Paul *the witness,* alive for the community while awaiting his death—even as he preaches the coming of the kingdom.

Suggested Readings

The following sources provide Lukan scholarship which will assist the reader of Acts of the Apostles in exploring questions which touch on Luke's portrait of Paul.

Boismard, M.-E., and A. Lamouille. *Les Actes des Deux Apôtres,* I, II, III. Études Bibliques. Nouvelle série No. 12. Paris: J. Gabalda, 1990.

Presently only available in French, it represents a reading of Acts based on a reconstituted Western text (*Codex Bezae,* as principal witness) which is taken as the earlier account of Acts, and the Alexandrine text (Vaticanus) taken as the later version. Readers with even basic knowledge of French will profit from reading the cross references to New Testament and Old Testament texts included in the pericope-by-pericope commentary on Acts in Volumes II and III. Volume IV (1994) in the same series is authored by Justin J. Taylor. He provides first-century historical, geographical, and political data which contextualizes the analysis of Acts undertaken in the first three volumes.

Bovon, François. *Luke the Theologian: Thirty-Three Years of Research (1950-1983).* Trans. Ken McKinney from *Luc le théologien* (Neuchtel-Paris: Delachaux & Niestlé, 1978). Princeton Theological Monograph Series 12. Allison Park, Penn.: Pickwick Publications, 1987.

This is a translation and revision of the French version, largely a survey of writing about Luke's theological themes: salvation history and eschatology, interpretation of Old Testament, Christology, Holy Spirit, salvation and its reception, and Church. Bibliographies include European as well as English-language resources.

Brawley, Robert L. *Centering on God: Method and Message in Luke-Acts.* Literary Currents in Biblical Interpretation. Louisville: Westminster/John Knox, 1990.

Brawley uses primarily a structuralist approach to reinterpret in Acts the characterization of Peter and Paul, the genres synthesized in the narrative of Luke-Acts, and the thematic oppositions which organize the book. Brawley retrieves those aspects of structuralism which have a direct bearing on the discussion of Luke's theology.

Bruce, F. F. *Paul: Apostle of the Heart Set Free.* Exeter: Paternoster Press, 1977/Grand Rapids, Mich.: Eerdmans, 1988.

This is a readable biographical synthesis of Paul's life, based on the narrative in Acts. References to the Pauline epistles corroborate Luke, according to Bruce's analysis. The volume treats geographical, cultural, and political data within the overall narrative, not as footnotes. Luke's theological perspective is not abstracted from Acts, but arises from the biographical treatment of Paul. Bibliographical references are dated, but Bruce's narrative itself is still clear and useful.

Cadbury, Henry J. "Acts and Eschatology." *The Background of the New Testament and Its Eschatology: In Honour of Charles Harold Dodd.* Ed. William David Davies and David Daube. Cambridge: Cambridge University Press, 1956 (300–21).

This classic essay is a good example of the perspective of Davies and Daube, as well. All three authors are reliable interpreters of the Lukan corpus within the context of New Testament theology in dialogue with its Jewish heritage. Their recognition of the importance of the Jewish milieu of the New Testament anticipated the scholarship of the 1980s.

Green, Joel B., and Michael C. McKeever. *Luke-Acts & New Testament Historiography.* Grand Rapids, Mich.: Baker Book House, 1994.

This bibliographical reference guide is part of an overall New Testament project undertaken by the Institute for Biblical Research. Designed for student researchers, the volume annotates over 500 English-language sources appearing in the last twenty-five years.

Hengel, Martin. *Between Jesus and Paul: Studies in the Earliest History of Christianity.* Trans. John Bowden from articles appearing in German periodicals 1971–1983. London: SCM Press, Ltd., 1983.

Hengel takes a position contrary to Conzelmann and others who dismiss Luke's accuracy as a geographer on the basis of Luke 17:11. Hengel maintains that Luke had accurate knowledge of the land of Palestine. Luke's geographical references in Acts and his familiarity with the Temple environs bespeak a reliability which was not exceeded by his own contemporaries who traveled the same routes from Jerusalem to Gaza, Joppa, Antipatris, and Caesarea. See especially "Luke the Historian and the Geography of Palestine in the Acts of the Apostles," 97–128.

Johnson, Luke T. *Acts of the Apostles.* Sacra Pagina Series 5. Daniel
 Harrington, S.J., ed. Collegeville, Minn.: Michael Glazier/The
 Liturgical Press, 1992.

This scholarly and readable commentary treats Acts as apologetic history whose "fictional shaping" reveals the literary and religious purposes of Luke. Each large narrative unit is broken down into a pericope-by-pericope commentary, with translation, notes, and references for each unit. In 500 pages he cites over 250 authors and integrates lexical, historical, literary, and theological material into accessible essays useful for preaching, teaching, and research.

Kurz, William S., S.J. *Reading Luke-Acts: Dynamics of Biblical Narra-*
 tive. Louisville, Kentucky: Westminster/John Knox Press, 1993.

This is not a chapter-by-chapter commentary, but rather a synthetic reading of sections of Luke and Acts taking the approach of literary criticism. Plotting, gaps, multiple narrative perspective and authorial commentary are the Lukan strategies Kurz highlights. He has valuable sections on the prologue to Luke as the "we"-narrator(s) in Acts. Notes and bibliography make this a useful resource, as well as model, for those interested in a literary-critical analysis of Scripture.

Neyrey, Jerome H., ed. *The Social World of Luke-Acts: Models for In-*
 terpretation. Peabody, Mass.: Hendrickson, 1991.

The essays are composed largely by members of the Social Study of the New Testament group of the Society of Biblical Literature and the Catholic Biblical Association. They cover such dynamics as honor and shame, communitarianism versus individualism, conflict and deviance, the urban versus the rural, Temple and household, patron-client relations, status, and ceremonies of inclusion.

Powell, Mark Allan. *What Are They Saying about Luke?* Mahwah:
 Paulist Press, 1989.

Powell provides a selective bibliography which illustrates current trends in Lukan scholarship. Using Conzelmann's *The Theology of St. Luke*

(1957, 1960) as a foil, Powell reviews more recent perspectives on Luke as historian, theologian, and artist, and on the composition of Luke's Gospel. Other issues require a consideration of questions which bridge the Gospel and the Acts of the Apostles: concerns of Luke's community, Christ and salvation, political and social issues (debates over the nature of Luke's political apology, call to revolution, plea for peace, concern for the disadvantaged, role of women, rich and poor), and the spiritual and pastoral concerns (salvation, Holy Spirit, community, prayer, teaching, and mission).

Richard, Earl, ed. *New Views on Luke and Acts*. Collegeville: The Liturgical Press, 1990.

The eleven essays in this volume come from members of the Luke-Acts Task Force of the Catholic Biblical Association. They deal with the religious and cultural setting of Luke-Acts, literary analysis of episodes, and theological themes of discipleship, God, Pentecost, and opposition to Paul. Contributors included Earl Richard, Marion L. Soards, Dennis M. Sweetland, Robert L. Mowery, Judette Kolasny, Thomas L. Brodie, Marie-Eloise Rosenblatt, and Richard J. Cassidy.

Segal, Alan F. *Paul the Convert: The Apostolate and Apostasy of Saul the Pharisee*. New Haven and London: Yale University Press, 1990.

This acclaimed biographical and social analysis by a Jewish scholar acknowledges that the epistles of Paul provide data which offer insight into the complexities of first century Judaism. Segal uses the theme of personal conversion as a description of the evolution taking place in Paul's society among both Jews and Gentiles. Segal assumes that Paul expresses his own mystical experience within Jewish biblical categories and communicates his message to Gentiles in language which represents Paul's interpretation of Torah. This book is both well-annotated and engagingly written.

Tajra, Harry W. *The Trial of St. Paul: A Juridical Exegesis of the Second Half of the Acts of the Apostles*. Tübingen: J.C.B. Mohr/Paul Siebeck, 1989.

This pericope-by-pericope commentary is sometimes uneven in its alternation between provision of historical or linguistic data and unanalytical paraphrase. Of use is its material on Roman law, social conventions in the Mediterranean, and economic conditions affecting sea voyages, and its cross-references with the classical literature on such personages as Festus, the Herods, Berenice, and the Roman emperors.

Winter, Bruce W., and Andrew D. Clarke, eds. *The Book of Acts in Its First Century Setting.* Vol. 1. Ancient Literary Setting. Grand Rapids, Mich.: Eerdmans, 1994.

This fourteen-author anthology grew out of a consultation of scholars at Cambridge. It is part of a larger project on Acts that comprises five other volumes: *Graeco-Roman Setting* (D. Gill and C. Gempf, eds.), *Paul in Roman Custody* (B. Rapske), *Palestinian Setting* (R. Bauckham, ed.), *Diaspora Setting* (I. Levinskaya), and *Theological Setting* (I. H. Marshall and D. Peterson, eds.).

Wuellner, Wilhelm, and Hayim Perelmuter. "Paul the Jew: Jewish-Christian Dialogue." *Center for Hermeneutical Studies.* Vol. 60. Twentieth Anniversary Symposium. Berkeley: Graduate Theological Union, 1990.

This volume, a set of resources rather than a lengthy study, includes several papers from the participants in a symposium on the relation of Paul to his Jewish background. Offered is a transcript of the dialogue and a course outline for adult education treating Paul, Church, and synagogue. A curriculum for a short study series for adults organizes themes in the Pauline Epistles, and provides directives for the facilitator. There are ample bibliographies on Paul, Pharisaism, first-century Judaism, Jewish-Christian scholarship on biblical issues in the New Testament, and problems of contemporary interpretation.

Subject Index

accusation vocabulary, 74
accusations against Paul,
    Stephen compared, 24
Agabus, 67, 68n.11
Agrippa, 9, 10, 85, 86
Ananias, 5, 10, 27-28, 71, 76-
    77, 83-84
    vision, 16, 84
    as witness, 3, 17
Antioch (Pisidia), Paul at, 10,
    15, 22, 31
    Paul's preaching at, 8, 15,
    32-36, 40
Antioch (Syria), 30-31, 32, 41
"apostle"
    Lukan definition of, 12
    term replaced by "witness," 17
Apostles, as witnesses, 7, 12
Aquila, 56
Ascension of Jesus (as temporal
    marker), 12, 34
Athens, 42, 53-55, 59-60

Barnabas, 12n.6, 30-31, 34-39,
    42n.2
    healing by, 45-46
    human identity of, 39, 40
    and mission to Gentiles, 30
    mission with Paul, 34-39

quarrel with Paul, 42
stoning of, 59
supporter of Paul in Jerusa-
    lem, 29
Berenice, 81
Beroea, 42, 51-53, 59

Caesar, Paul's appeal to, 80, 88
Caesarea, 5, 11
    linked to "witness," 10, 10n.6
    Paul at, 9, 29, 66, 74-81, 86-87
    Paul in prison at, 2
    on Paul's missionary circuit, 2
    Peter at, 4
Christians, Jewish, 62, 68-74
    chronology, 56n.24
    Lukan replacement for, 10-11
Church, the
    at Jerusalem, 8, 27, 29, 68-69
    official policy toward not
        widely known, 68
    outreach to Gentiles, 6, 8, 9,
        11, 14-16, 30-31, 57n.27, 68
    outreach to Jews, 57n.27
    persecutions against, 27, 29
    and witnessing, 8, 9, 38
circumcision, 68, 69n.13, 70
civil forum, 23, 36, 38, 43-45,
    49, 52, 53, 56

103

Author Index

Scripture Citation Index